I0150554

Black Gold

*Commemorating the Anniversary
of the
Auchengeich Colliery Disaster*

This book is dedicated to the forty-seven men who lost their lives on September, 18th, 1959.

Never shall they go down the mine like then

First published in 2012.

A catalogue record of this book is available from
the British Library.

ISBN 978-1-907463-07-5

Contents

Remembering

Story Contributors
(Special Thanks)

With thanks to those who have contributed
their real-life account of what happened that
day on September, 18th, 1959.

Anne Wharrie
Elisabeth Howieson
Erica Windsor Nunn
Gordon Muir
Irene Murphy
Isobel Wharrie
James Whyte
Jean Skilling
Jeanie Marshall
John McPhee
Joseph Milligan
Loretta Wotherspoon
Marion McWhinnie
Mary Moodey
Neil Milligan
Pat Doyle
Samual Barr
Samual Green
Tom Skilling
Tom Whiteside
Willie S. Stewart
Rita McNaughton
Alison Schuchs
Trish Borgogno
Archie Downie
Bill Ewing

Carol Quinn
Joanne Reilly
Liz Cullen
Robert Armour
Tom McLelland

Special thanks to Patricia Pearson for her
childhood story.

Special mention to Robert Harvey, Joan Hill,
Jack Duffy, Andy Whitelaw, Ian Lowe, Jean
Mitchell, Mr Stevens, Billy Maxwell, Gerry
Stark, Dr George Jamieson, John Docherty,
Anna Atkinson, Irene Docherty, James
Docherty, Alan Bridges, Ally Wharrie, Elsie
Howieson, Gerry Farrell, Catherine Farrell,
Frankie Farrell, Liz Cullen, Eileen Martin,
Johnny Templeton, Adam Smith, Rob Conn,
Margaret Chalmers, Lorraine Legg, Bill Adair,
Ray Martin and Joan Clark.

Special thank you to Eric Savage.

BLACK GOLD

(words and music by Ray Martin)

50 YEARS HAS GONE AND THE MEMORY
LINGERS ON
FOR THE MEN THAT GAVE THIER LIVES AT
AUCHENGEICH
LEAVING CHILDREN AND THEIR WIVES BEHIND
FOR THE RICH BLACK GOLD WAS TO BE MINED

AND THE COST WE´LL NEVER KNOW
OUR LOVE WILL ALWAYS SHOW
OUR GRIEVING IS SO SLOW

LOOK AT ME AND TELL ME THIS WILL EVER
END
FIFTY YEARS I HAVE SPENT THINKING OF YOU
FRIEND
COULD IT BE ONE DAY THAT WE WILL MEET
AGAIN
BUT NEVER SHALL THEY GO DOWN THE MINE
LIKE THEN
OH NEVER SHALL THEY GO DOWN THE MINE
LIKE THEN

AS THE YEARS ROLL BY I LOOK UP TO THE SKY
AND THINK OF THOSE NOT FEW AND GOD I
PRAY
HELP EASE MY PAIN, BREAK THIS STRAIN
GIVE ME ONE MORE DAY TO THINK OF YOU

I SHALL NEVER BE ALONE
AS EACH DAY THAT I HAVE GROWN
I HAVE THOUGHT OF YOU AND KNOW, KNOW

REPEAT CHORUS

TIME AND PAST ROLLS ALONG
THE RICH BLACK GOLD HAS ALMOST GONE
AS THE DAYS GO BY
I HOLD MY HEAD UP HIGH
I THINK OF YOU AND THEN I FORCE A SMILE

SO SAD TO TELL MY TALE
NOW I'M OLD AND FRAIL
THE STILLNESS WE HAVE SHARED, SHARE

REPEAT CHORUS

FIFTY YEARS HAS GONE AND THE MEMORY
LINGERS ON
FOR THE MEN THAT GAVE THEIR LIVES AT
AUCHENGEICH

To listen to this track please go to:
www.blackgoldonline.co.uk

Black Gold

Black for the day that was
18th September, 1959.

Gold for the value of the forty-seven brave
men who lost their lives that day.

BLACK GOLD
INTRODUCTION

A couple of independent creative individuals were brought to the attention of the Auchengeich disaster by Joan Clark – Social Convener of the Auchengeich Miners' Club.

The main objective was to highlight and hopefully raise awareness of the pit disaster through creative works and the world wide web. Its primary aim was to reach comrades and associates of the disaster from as far away as possible. The plan was initially to target a nationwide audience but this grew to a mailing and contact list from Coatbridge to Canada .

The response the Black Gold project received was astonishing. Ex-miners who hadn't seen each other since the disaster were brought back in touch. Correspondence from people who knew each other but had no idea that they were connected to the disaster in some way and messages from people as far away as Australia.

The Black Gold project also wrapped up in no time the services of Scottish pop/soul band, Shifter X. Lead singer/songwriter, Ray Martin was given the task of producing a music soundtrack that would be complimentary and touching at the same time. A superb haunting but moving track was recorded by the band for Black Gold's web presentation and was quickly followed by a tremendous track that received radio play with resounding praise.

The project began to grow and yet we still didn't have a title for the project. We couldn't label ourselves with the name Auchengeich because we are actually a separate entity from Auchengeich; although our purpose was to raise awareness of the Auchengeich mining disaster.

It was thanks to Ray Martin from Shifter X that we now have the project name of *Black Gold.*

INTRODUCTION

There are many dates in our history where we can say, "I remember where I was the day that happened," and in other calendar events – mainly sporting and entertainment – we often hear the chuckling of, "I was there."

There are many private dates in our history that we remember with fondness: weddings, the day you left school, your first job et cetera but sadly, there are dates – that for whatever reason – are stamped in our minds, leaving a reminding print that never leaves us.

That day for many, occurred one early shift on September 18th 1959.

Five decades, to be exact, and although life and times have moved on quite considerably, for a large chunk of the Auchengeich community, life would never be the same again.

Time has virtually stood still for the relatives of those who lost a loved one in what sadly turned out to be one of Scotland 's worst-ever disasters of any kind.

September 18th was to be like any other shift – or so we thought. That day just happened to be the day that left a huge God-awful wound without a healing after-scar across a small area; so small you could hear your neighbour boiling the kettle and the creek of floor boards as they rose for their early morning chores. So small that everyone lived like an extended family so it was even more devastating for all the family members and neighbours alike when disaster struck on what has become a landmark date: 18th September 1959.

Forty-seven men would go through their normal shift-to-shift ritual at home; the dear wife tucking the flask and *chits* into her hard-working husband's bag and off he would go into the dark...literally speaking. Mothers, girlfriends, aunts and sisters would probably have gone through that same daily and nightly scenario. The common ground all had on this fateful day was that all of them would be expecting to return home from their daily grind down the pit: forty-seven men never did.

At around 7am that morning of September 18th, an electrical failure sparked a blaze; the smoke and fumes from the fire brought about horrific difficulties to the men already in their bogies as they made their way down underground to begin their shifts. The fire entrapped the miners and God only knows how they must have felt. The sheer panic must have been all too overwhelming as the surface was filled with fear and sheer panic.

Only if you were there could you begin to imagine what horror was unfolding in front of you. What if fate had dealt another hand? What if there wasn't an electrical failure? Those questions must have been a fragment of the many other queries from the surviving families and for the friends who were left behind with the pain of an absent buddy.

The morning unfolded with news spilling out onto the community and beyond. As of any event that didn't yet have facts, a lot of rumours began to spread throughout; some not so bad but some mostly of absolute horror. Kids would be in school as that morning grew into lunchtime and of course in those days the mere scrappings of communication were left to the emergency people and those lucky enough to have afforded a land line phone connection.

Much of the news filtered onto the streets as the patrons of the community ran back and forth, with and in search of vital information. Mothers, wives, fathers, uncles and brothers all desperate to get their hands on any good news. Any slither of a relief would be the perfect medicine but sadly, the death toll would escalate to a catastrophic height.

Over one-thousand people from the mining community and around began to congregate around the pit for a hopeful announcement. An announcement that all had prayed for: that the accident was just a fire and that no-one was hurt. Those threaded glimmers of hope were quickly dashed when it was agreed the pit was to be flooded to try and distinguish the flames. By then the locals got known to the fact that some men were indeed reported missing and *unaccounted* for.

The flooding of the pit decision was not taken lightly. As for any rescue attempt, the well-being of the victims and the stranded are paramount but it was a decision, nevertheless, that was carried out. One man did survive but forty-seven miners perished and as a result, the thriving community was thrust upon the map of a growing list of known disasters worldwide in one short moment of time.

The media descended onto the community and one-by-one, the strokes of journalists' pens began to form the frame of a horrendous real-life event; the Auchengeich Colliery became a household name and for all the sad reasons.

That day gave birth to what we now refer to as: *The Auchengeich Mining Disaster.*

Musicians have recorded their works about it. Writers have written about it. Poets have prose'd it. Many reporters have reported it. Bloggers have blogged about it but many have remained silent on it.

The Auchengeich mining disaster has left scars in the physical sense but mentally: many have lost their voice or chose not to air their experience, vocally.

It is very easy to understand why.

Things in Scotland are small-ish in terms of population, communities and living dwellings and when things are small they tend to be tight and nowhere could you find a more close-knit environment than the families of hard-working patrons of that community.

Miners and their families are especially close-knit so when the disaster unfolded on that grey September day, over fifty-years ago, there was an impact that rippled through the communities and spread to other close-by villages and towns.

If there was an event that put this tiny village on the map then this was sadly it.

Some villages and towns become worldly known if one of the members in its community went on to Hollywood status. Some mining villages – and there are many in Scotland – who have produced top football players and managers: Jock Stein and Bill Shankly come to mind. Auchengeich became a name across the globe and touched hearts on the other side; as far away as America , Canada and Australia simply because of the disaster.

What can you write that hasn't already been written about the Auchengeich disaster? What words can you say that can be a source of comfort for the families and where do you begin with a book project like this that the remaining families can cherish and pass down generations to come? It has to be the most difficult true-life story to tell from a keyboard.

No-one can write this story the way the people who were part of the disaster can tell it; this is why we leave this book's contents to the people who know it better than any of us: the people who were there and the people who lost a loved one.

People like Isobel Wharrie *(nee Green)* who at 14-years-old made her way home from school to be approached by someone in the street and told her that her dad and brother were killed in the pit disaster; only to find out later and much to her and her family's relief, that her dad and brother were in fact very much alive.

There are people to this very day who cannot and will not speak about the disaster; almost like the day stood still for many. There are others, like James Whyte, who recalls the great characters of those days which you can gather when you read his passage, that he had wonderful memories working at the *Geich*.

In words...

In Words...

By Anne Wharrie

I was working at McLaughlan's, the bookmaker, in Charing Cross, Glasgow. It was a normal morning until the girl who worked next to me told me of a mining disaster; she said it was in a mine called, "Auch, *Auchensomething::.*"

I left my desk, rushed out and bought a paper and read about the disaster in the Auchengeich mine where my father, brother and uncle – as well as a few close family friends – worked.

It stated in that paper that my dad had been brought up the mine and that he was alive. Obviously I was devastated and didn't know what to think. I was immediately sent home by my boss. On the way home to Glenboig I was told that both my dad and my brother were dead.

Panicking and very upset I got to my home in Marnoch Drive, Glenboig *(home of my parents, Tam and Maggie Green)* to face a barrage of reporters and photographers.

Expecting to be told the worst possible news when I entered the house, it was then that I found out that both my brother and my father were alive for sure, and my Uncle Sam had taken the day off to go to the races at Ayr, thankfully.

My brother, Sam was lucky enough not to have gone down the mine and was not involved in the disaster. My Dad was upstairs in his bed resting and the relief swept over me; that was until word began to filter through to us that the news from the pit was not good.

My Father had lost two of his closest friends, Jimmy Devine and Pete McMillan and after a while he realized that he was indeed the only man to come out of that pit alive. If it had not been for one of the rescue team standing on his face he would never been found in time. As my sister Elsie has said in her contribution to the book: "My father hardly ever spoke of his experience down that mine, only to say that, 'It was not my time to go.'"

He was devastated; losing all his friends and work-mates.

Up until the day he died, in the mid-seventies, he was always very quiet and subdued on the run up to, and over the anniversary of that fateful day on 18th September, 1959.

Years later after my father died I found out purely by chance that my neighbour in Holytown, Mr John Grant, whom I had known for over thirty years, was in fact one of the rescue team that had helped to bring my father to safety all those years earlier.

Sadly since then, John has also passed away, but he will always be a hero, in my eyes.

Anne *(Green)* Wharrie
Aged 18 at the time of the disaster.

In Words...

By Elisabeth (Elsie Green) Howieson

My father was the sole survivor of the disaster. On that day I left home to travel to work in Collins sewing factory in Milnebank Street, Glasgow.

At lunchtime, around 12:30pm, I went round to the corner shop for something for my lunch. I heard people talking about a pit disaster; then I heard the word *Auchengeich.* That was where my father, brother and uncle all worked. I had to get home.

My cousin came and picked me up and we travelled home together on the bus. It was when I got home *(the street was covered in cars, belonging to all the reporters and photographers)* that I found out that my father was alive; although he had been down the pit.

My brother, Sam was ready to go down in the next cage, so was luckily not involved and my Uncle Sam Green had taken the day off to go to Ayr races. I was allowed upstairs to see my father for a few minutes and was then ushered back downstairs by my mother to allow my father to rest.

In the years that followed after my father being the sole survivor, he hardly spoke of what he had been through. On the anniversaries of that day he was very quiet and I could see that he was thinking of all his mates that had died.

Elisabeth (Elsie Green) Howieson
Aged 25 at the time of the disaster.

In Words...

By Erica Windsor Nunn

My late husband and I were both stationed at RAF Leuchars, on Battle of Britain Day, 18th September 1959. Myself in Air Traffic Control and him in Mountain Rescue. It also happened to be our wedding day; just four of us.

We were married at Leuchars Church but before the marriage, the vicar discovered that our best man's father had been in the disaster and insisted that Johnny was okay and his father – who had been involved – was safe.

Of course, the first thing we all did was pray for everyone and thank God for people's safety *(and sorrow)* and since then, I always remember the tragedy and say a little prayer. We all had to go straight back on duty and I worked until after midnight but Johnny and Tom had quite a *'heavy'* night, if I remember rightly, with relief and gratitude.

It was a strange day and I was widowed *(with two babies)* three years later but a day I will never forget for so many reasons.

Erica Windsor Nunn

In Words...

By Gordon Muir

At the time in question I was a 16-year-old office boy at Auchengeich Colliery and living in Kirkintilloch. On this day I was walking down to the colliery from Chryston after coming off the bus when I noticed smoke coming out of No:2 pit shaft.

On arrival at the colliery, I was informed that forty-eight men were trapped underground by a fire which we later learned had allegedly been caused by a fan belt. Only one man, Tom Green, survived.

As a young boy I had never come across anything like this before as there seemed to be miners everywhere all anxious to assist in trying to rescue their comrades. Also numerous medical staff/police were in attendance; plus of course, newspaper reporters were also beginning to arrive at the pit-head.

As the morning went by, more Mines Rescue Personnel and miners from out-with the immediate area arrived equipped with breathing apparatus and they seemed to be continually descending/ascending the shaft.

More officials also arrived at the colliery in an attempt to find a solution as to how to extinguish the fire and bring the trapped men out safely.

By this time, word had got round the various nearby towns and villages with families of the trapped miners beginning to arrive at the colliery for news updates.

Also, I recall the Salvation Army mobile canteen arriving at the colliery which remained open all the time the rescue was taking place in order to cater for the needs of relatives and rescue personal etc.

The colliery had a brick outbuilding behind the office which garaged the colliery office car and dumper truck. This had been made into a makeshift mortuary once the bodies had been brought to the surface some days later; and I recall having to take a telephone message over to the pathologist; I think his name was Doctor Imrie and to this date, can still remember the smell of burning flesh from the bodies.

Gordon Muir
Relationship To Disaster: Colliery Employee.

In Words...

By Irene Murphy, nee Docherty

I was the youngest of eight children. Four boys; Edward, Andrew, Archie & James, and four girls; Ann, Margaret, Janet & myself. Although I was only eight-years-old on that terrible day I can still remember it. I don't think anyone who was involved with the disaster will ever forget it.

They slept in that morning; my father Andrew Whyte Docherty who was forty-three-years-old, and my eighteen-year-old brother, Edward. Any other day my father would have cycled to work, but rather than go late he decided to accept a lift from Edward on his motorbike, *(although he hated motorbikes and didn't like my brother having one).*

Miners were normally superstitious, when they slept in they took it as a *'sign'* and they just wouldn't go to work that day, but I think the fact that they had been on strike for a few days, and they couldn't afford any more time off, was the deciding factor.

I wasn't at school that day, I had earache and my mother and I were the only ones in the house. Everyone else had gone off to work or school.

My mother looked out of the window and saw my granny running in and out of my aunties' houses. My mother's sisters all lived in the same street in Waterside, Kirkintilloch: No's 5, 6, 7 & 10, to be exact, with my granny living just round the corner. They were very close, as were all the kids. Our best friends were our cousins.

My mother said, "Something is wrong, I wonder why they aren't coming in here."

Just then my aunty came running down the path with my granny running after her.

My aunty said, "Something has happened up at the pit, Janet, it was on the news."

Of course my mother was in a panic. She didn't know who was involved, my father and brother were both working that day.

Thankfully, Edward was alright, he had to go back and get his tag, and he hadn't gone down the pit with my father.

The word spread like wildfire, and the house filled up with family and friends.

My brothers and sisters were sent home from work and school, and some of them went up to the pit-head.

I don't think we believed that my father wasn't coming home, there was still hope. When the word came that they were going to flood the pit, everyone was devastated. I can just remember that my mother didn't open her eyes or speak to anyone until after the funeral, she was in total shock. I was scared she wouldn't speak again.

I can name so many of the men and boys who died on that day, but until now they have been just that: names. Now, for the first time in fifty-years, people will hear stories about the men behind the names, and get to know something about them, and I look forward to reading the other families' stories.

My father was a good, hard-working family man. I have memories of him playing the accordion at my birthday parties, and at New Year parties; of standing on the pedal of his bike and being pushed; of him lifting me up with one hand to touch the ceiling, with my mother fussing that he would drop me. But my memories are the memories of an eight-year-old child, because I didn't get to know him as an adult.

That day our lives changed forever, but in those days counselling wasn't offered, although I'm sure our family would have benefited from it.

We have never missed the memorial services, but sadly our numbers are dwindling, as my mother, Edward, Margaret & Janet are no longer with us.

Irene Murphy
nee Docherty

In Words...

By Isobel (Green) Wharrie

On the day of the disaster I was at Clifton High School, Coatbridge. During the dinner break I was down the street when I spotted a poster on a news stand outside the newsagents which read: *'Lanarkshire Pit Disaster'.*

A shiver went through me but I thought it couldn't be Auchengeich where my dad and brother worked.

I gave it no more thought and continued on with my day.

On my way home from school around 4pm, I got off the bus to go and collect my grandfather's shopping, when I was approached by someone telling me to go straight home as both my dad and my brother were dead. I was frightened of even thinking of going home to face my mother if this was true.

I headed straight for my grandfather's house. It was when I got there that my Uncle Sam Green, who himself was supposed to have been working down the pit that day but taken the day off, told me that they *(being my dad and brother)* were alive.

My brother had not yet gone into the pit when the alarm sounded trouble down below. My dad had been brought up alive.

After what I had been told I didn't believe him

at first, by this time I was hysterical. My uncle then walked me home and all I can remember about that was the amount of people standing around with cameras and notebooks. They were all trying to get into my house with me when I entered. I then raced upstairs to see for myself that my dad was alive. It was such a relief to know that they were there talking to me after I had been told that they were dead. I was fourteen-years-old at this time and probably knew a lot more of my father's friends but the two names that stick in my head are Pete McMillan and wee Jimmy Devine who along with his family were regular visitors to our family home.

Isobel (Green) Wharrie
Aged 14 at the time of the disaster.

In Words...

By James Whyte

I worked in the *'Geich'* from 1950 – 1958 as a shotfirer and I have many memories of working in that happy but ill-fated pit. There were two pits – the square pit and the round pit. The round pit was the up cast or the return shaft for the ventilation. The square pit was the down cast.

I remember Tammy Green as I fired many shots for him and I am surprised that he survived as he had chest troubles due to dust.

Aaron and Robert Price were brothers and were staunch masons. I had many discussions with them about the Masonic Order. They were mine drivers.

James Devine, known as Devanny, and Mick Fleming were shotfirers. They were an irrepressible pair; full of fun. Mick was bald and Devanny called him Danny Druff.

Underground, they sat together and tormented the Wood boys by crawling up in darkness and throwing stone dust on them, but the Wood boys got a water hose and unexpectedly drenched them.

Dick Hamilton, who stayed close to them in Bridgend village, which was a collection of miners' rows was also a butt of their jokes. Devanny and Danny Druff delighted in telling everyone how Dick climbed onto the roof on

Christmas Eve to call down the chimney to his children and fell off!

Frank Fisher, shotfirer, worked beside me in Waterside Colliery where I was a pit drawer.

Gerald Martin, who was also a shotfirer had been a policeman in Manchester before he entered the mines. He lived with his parents in Chryston. I was his friend and played many games of snooker with him.

Andrew McKenna, shotfirer, was involved in a fatal accident in which Robert McGuiness was struck by flying debris and killed.

Robert McCoid lived with his parents in Ardholm Street in Shettleston. We travelled together to the pit in the morning. He was a heavy smoker but gave it up when Hugh Dalton, the Chancellor, doubled the price of a packet of cigarettes.

Geordie McIntosh had a serious accident when we were travelling out the haulage road at the end of the shift. He was caught by a rake of hutches and was trapped underneath them.

Alex Smith known as Pinty Smith was my brother-in-law and was married to my sister, Cathy. He is shown on a picture on the website.

I had a passing acquaintance with most of the men who died and found them to be a very friendly crowd of men.

It was a pleasure to work in that pit and it was a pity to miss a shift.

I was working in the Lumloch Colliery underground on the day of the accident. I remember vividly receiving the news. I have never forgotten the sadness I felt on discovering that so many of my comrades had been involved.

Since both pits were joined by an underground safety road which had been driven during the war, the smoke from the fire came through to the Lumloch necessitating stoppings being built to seal of the workings and I was transferred to Ayrshire where I still reside.

To those who lost fathers and grandfathers in that terrible tragedy I would like you to know that they were a wonderful bunch of men and you should be proud of them and respect their memories. They did not deserve to die like that.

James Whyte
90-years-old

In words...

By Jean Jaap, nee Skilling

I remember getting wakened up by my mother and she said there had been an accident at the pit my dad worked in. My mum went across the road to see if Mr Connelly or Mr Cowan had seen my dad but they hadn't seen him and my mum said, "Your dad will probably be helping."

But as the day went on there was still no news of my dad and I was sent to Burnbank, Hamilton to get my dad's sister and when she came to the door she said, "I bet it's our Wullie." But anyway she came back home to my mum's house with me and we waited for news of my dad.

It was later at night when the Salvation Army people came to tell us that my dad was one of the men that were missing. It really was terrible hearing those words and then the photographers came to the door to get photos of my dad, but they were hunted away from our door by friends and neighbours. It was three days later when we found out what had happened and my oldest brother had to go and identify my dad. I can remember him coming back; he was in a terrible state as we all were.

My father had been sick all week and had decided that morning that he was well enough to work and I can remember my mum saying to my dad, "Don't go, it's only one shift." But my dad said, "It will pay the rent." That's what kind of man my dad was. He was a great dad. I was 21-years-old at the time.

Jean Jaap
nee Skilling *(daughter of William Skilling)*

In Words...

By Jeanie Marshall

I recall that day. I was in school when the news came there was a fire at the pit. Some of the boys at school said that someone had probably dropped a cigarette; no-one had any idea how bad it was.

My dad took it bad as he had given them all their lamps that day as he worked in the lamp cabin.

I did not know 'till I got home that my big brother, George was one of the men trapped. He was twenty-one and his daughter, Marion was five-weeks-old and getting christened on the Sunday.

I was sent to stay with my sister-in-law's family in Bonnybridge 'till the Sunday when I came home for the christening. Marion was christened in the house as the Minister said it would be better for all concerned.

Our house was never empty; there was always people coming and going. Because of Marion we had reporters wanting pictures.

It was like a bad dream that never seamed to end.

I would not wish that on anyone.

Jeanie Marshall
nee Jackson

In Words...

On that day we lost a father, an uncle, a brother, a cousin, a grandfather and a friend.

The unknown Miner

In words...

By James McPhee

On that awful day, 18th September 1959, I received a telephone call at work from my wife to tell me of the disaster at Auchengeich pit, where my father, James McPhee, worked as a shotfirer.

When I arrived at my parent's home, my uncles, dad's brothers, had already been to the pit and confirmed that dad was one of the men who had been killed.

My brother and I never saw dad's body after the disaster because his brothers identified him and advised us to remember him as we last saw him, which was kindly, since he was not dad as we had known him.

My mother and the family were in shock. At the age of fifty-four our dad had been killed in one of the worst mining disasters.

My mother was now a widow, we were left without a father, and our little children, whom he loved so much, were left without grandpa.

My dad was a lover of the works of Robert Burns and was often called upon to 'address the haggis' at Burn's Suppers.

He was cheerful and articulate, well-thought of by all who knew him. He was sorely missed.

James McPhee

In words...

By Joseph Milligan

In 1959 I was living in the miners' rows at 1 East Gartferry Road, Bridgend. My house was the first one in Bridgend and was nearest to the Auchengeich pit entrance. It was just across the road from the Miners' Welfare and the shops which served the village.

I had previously worked in Auchingeich from 1942 until 1946 but from then I had worked at Bedlay Colliery near Glenboig.

On 18th September 1959, although I was on the back shift, I was up and about early. It was a nice bright morning. My wife was getting my five-year-old son ready for school. He attended Bridgend Primary School which was just a few hundred yards along the road from the village.

At one point, maybe around 8.00 am, my wife said that there were a lot of people standing across the road near to the Welfare and the shops. I went outside and asked someone what was happening. They told me that something had happened over at the pit and that some men were trapped underground. I knew that my father, Duncan Milligan, and his brother, my Uncle Joe, were probably working in the pit on the day shift so I was concerned enough to go straight over to the colliery.

When I got over to the pit I seem to recall that it did not appear to be too busy at that point.

Certainly I do not remember many people being about.

I went straight to the lamp cabin and spoke to the lampman whom I knew but whose name I have forgotten. He told me that there was a fire underground in the Round Pit and that some miners were trapped. He also told me that other men were waiting at the pit head to see if they could go down and mount a rescue. The lampman knew that my father was underground and he did not refuse my request for a helmet and lamp. I learned later on that my Uncle Joe was off that day and was not underground.

I went straight from the lamp cabin to the pit head. There were other men there who were ready to go underground.

Just at that point I felt a tap on my shoulder. It was the pit manager, Mr. Smellie. He basically asked where I was going.

I told him that I was trying to get down the pit because by dad and uncle were down there. He asked their names and was able to tell me that my father was down in the Square Pit (non-disaster mine) and that my uncle was not down the pit at all.

He then asked me if I worked at Auchingeich. I told him that I had worked there years ago although I was now working in Bedlay.

He basically told me that it was more than his job was worth to let me go down the mine. He told me to go down the stairs, return my helmet and lamp and go home.

I returned the helmet and lamp but did not go home. I definitely wanted to find out that my father was safe.

Whilst I was waiting at the pit it began to get busy. The Mines' Rescue came from Coatbridge. Soon the press and television arrived. I also remember the Salvation Army being there.

Very quickly people realize the seriousness of the incident. News spread that the men who had been trapped underground were almost certainly dead having been overcome. At that point, however, nobody knew how many men were actually involved. It was only later on that day that we eventually learned that forty-seven of our comrades had died. I was shocked as were all who were there at the time.

I knew personally a lot of the men who died, and their families, because they lived beside me in Bridgend and in the surrounding villages.

I am now eighty-five and had worked in the pits for forty years. This was easily the worst incident in the Scottish coalfields during my time in the mining industry.

Joseph Milligan

In words...

By Loretta Wotherspoon

I am the daughter of Joseph McDonald who died in the Auchengeich Disaster. On the morning of the accident, my sisters, Sadie and Anna, were off to work as usual.

My twin brother, Lawrence and I went to school at St. Ninian's old school in Kirkintilloch.

My mother was at home in Auchinairn with my young sister, Rose Maria.

Everything at school was normal that morning. We were not in school very long when we were told to go out to the playground.

I remember that some rumours had started that there had been an accident at the pit and some of the children were upsetting another child, Janet Docherty, saying that her father had been killed. I remember her being in the middle of a group of children crying. I said to the other children to leave her alone and took her away from the group and telling her that everything would be alright.

Shortly after we were told to return to our classrooms. Our teacher made no mention of an accident but dismissed us and told us we had to go home.

My brother and I thought this was great, getting sent home early from school. We were 9-years-old and free from school for the rest of the day.

When we arrived home the house was full; my sisters had heard of the accident in Glasgow and had returned from work, my aunt and uncle and brother-in law were there.

It was then that I realized that something was terribly wrong. My sister, Sadie was hysterical and the family doctor, Dr. Dunlop had been called to the house.

No information was coming through from the pit. We never had a telephone or a car in those days. A despatch rider arrived at home and informed us that my father was okay and was working with the rescue teams, but my mother did not believe him as she said that my father would have got word to us somehow. One or two days later, I cannot remember which, we had no sense of time, the despatch rider returned to inform my mother that there had been a mistake and that my father had in fact been in the disaster.

The days that followed were dreadful, waiting for the men to be brought up from the pit.

My mother was very upset at not being able to bring my father's body home or have his coffin in the Church overnight before the funeral.

My father was laid to rest in The Auld Aisle cemetery, Kirkintilloch, close to Janet Docherty's father, Andrew Docherty.

Loretta Wotherspoon
nee McDonald

In words...

By Marion McWhinne

I can only say what I remember of that day on 18th September, 1959. I had been on a night duty as I was nursing, and was in my bed in the morning, when I received a phone call from my sister-in-law, Sally, from Springburn.

She told me it had been on the news that something had gone wrong at the *'Geich'* – an accident.

That was about nine or ten o'clock. A while later, my daughter, Isobel *(just turned 13)*, came in from school saying, "There's been an accident at daddy's pit!"

After she got into the house, she said with some relief, "daddy's boots are here, he's not down the pit."

My husband, Dave Gray, had days when he was in the pit and days when he wasn't and his pit boots were sometimes left in the house if he wasn't needing them that day.

It's hard to say how I felt that day, as when someone tells you that something like that has happened, and your husband is there, it's hard to describe those feelings. I felt a chill deep inside, but all I felt I could do was wait; as no-one had any answers about what had actually happened. All I could think of was Dave, my Dave; was he alright?

About 3.30pm, one of the other miners came to the door and told me that Dave was okay and not to worry. Dave would be home as soon as he could, but had things to sort out. It was about 2am the following morning that Dave came home in a dreadful state. It is difficult to describe him: poor colour, dreadful state, with a foolscap list in his hand, of all the men who were lost that day. Dave 's job was to give the men their 'tickets' detailing where they went on shift and he carried that thought with him for the couple of years after that until he died. Dave washed, changed and relaxed as far as he could for a couple of hours and was picked up again about 6am by his manager to go back to work. I remember him going to work with his manager each day, taking readings of gas levels in the flooded pit at the Geich.

That's my main memories of that day. I was so relieved when Dave was safe, and so very sorry for those others who had lost loved ones; people I never knew. It did have a lasting effect on Dave, as he struggled to recover from the loss of those men at the Geich that day.

Marion McWhinne
(Gray at time of incident).

In Words...

By Mary (Green) Moodey

My father, Thomas Green was the only survivor of the pit disaster. My memories of the Auchengeich mine disaster started with a phone call from a very distant relative who lived in Hamilton, Ontario, around 40-miles from where I lived; having moved to Canada years earlier.

He told us that he had heard about a mine disaster and had heard the name of Thomas Green, aged fifty-two, mentioned.

He thought that the disaster was at the Kirkintilloch mine and asked if we knew where my family members worked.

Of course, in 1959 the internet did not exist, telephones were common in Canada but not in the mining villages of Scotland so the only means of fast communication was by telegram.

We contacted a local radio station and finally found out that the disaster was indeed at Auchengeich, the mine where my father worked.

At that time we did not know the extent of the disaster or who was involved in it, because my brother and my uncle worked there too, but were not involved in the tragedy. It was two or three days later when we heard that my father was in fact in the mine at the time but he had somehow survived.

The weeks and months that followed revealed the total story and that my father had been the sole survivor as well as being *'The Forgotten Miner'*, because he had been the lucky one to survive he did not receive any of the benefits that the families of those who lost their lives did. He was never able to return to the job he loved and the only work he knew but he still had a young family and a wife to support.

Mary (Green) Moodey
Aged 23 at the time of the disaster.

In words...

By Neil Milligan

My wife, with our two children, Liz (6) and Duncan (3 months) were on holiday at Rothesay on the day of the disaster. We read it on the bill poster for the local evening paper as we were heading back to our holiday digs. My father, Duncan worked in the mine so it was the worst possible news for me.

I immediately tried to phone my parents but could not make contact and the operator said all the phones had been commandeered by the emergency services. We then just threw all our things together and caught the next ferry up to Wemyss Bay then on to St Enoch station. As we had a huge pram, I put all the bags and cases in it and ran with it to our home in the Gorbals. Margaret took the bus with the children. As soon as I got home I tried phoning my parents again *(who lived in Timbertown)* but still could not get through. I tried the operator again but was told no contact with the area could be made.

We decided we would have to travel out to the village but when we got there it was like a ghost town and my old family home was locked up. All this time I was hoping my father's luck had not run out. As a Gordon Highlander he had fought in the Great War and was wounded and gassed at Ypres or on the Somme. He had also been taken prisoner by the Germans but was freed by the Canadians – who then threatened to kill the three Tommies because they thought they were Germans masquerading as British soldiers with their *'funny'* uniforms.

After the war my father returned to work in the Redding colliery at Polmont and left again just before the disaster there in 1923 *(which was caused by flooding)* to work at Auchengeich. In the late 30s he was involved in a bad accident when his two mates, Alex Ryan and Terry McManus were killed and he was badly injured trying to save them.

All the time since I'd heard of the disaster, all the foregoing was going through my mind. Had my dad's luck finally run out? Was this the end of many dangerous events in war and in coal mining that had been his life so far?

We headed down to the pit where hundreds of people had gathered, along with police, medical services, reserve workers and the media. It was a haunting sight, seeing all these folk, just waiting in silence and praying that their loved ones were safe.

To my utter amazement and joy, we found my father safe with my mother. He told me that he and others had walked underground to Western Auchengeich *(Lumloch)* and were brought safely to the surface there. So his luck had not run out!

Many others were not so lucky. My school mate Donald Weir *(who played football with Celtic);* Mick and Mouse Fleming, whose brother Tommy did not work at the pit again, and many others too numerous to mention.

They all died because they lived to dig coal and a faulty ventilator belt killed them when it was put there to keep them alive.

Neil Milligan

In words...

By Pat Doyle

There are times in my story that I can't remember. Things, such as, for example: I can see Alma Fagin, the bus conductress, sitting on the seat as you go in the bottom deck on your right; I knew all the men who would get on the bus. Stirling Rd, Townhead; Alexander Park and the top of Riddre Hill; Stepps and Muirhead then Chryston but I can't remember their faces or where they would be seated on the bus.

Same as in the canteen, the same in the baths, also pit-head, and on the cage as well and the pit bottom. I think this is very strange, but they say you can't remember everything you see or hear. So here I would like to say, "I'm open to contradiction and corrections that might take place in changes to it."

You often hear the question, "Where were you when...?"

Knockshinnock – I was at School.

Cheapside St fire where fifteen firemen perished and the Ibrox disaster were 66 died. Also, 9/11, U.S.A. I know exactly where I was in detail.

On Friday the 18th Sept 1959 at 7.10 in the morning, we were waiting for our oversman,

Sanny Deans, to detail each man to his day's work. This done, we got ready to send up the stone waste from the Backshift Brushers from Friday the 11th of Sept. Remember the strike.

As we were getting ready the phone rang from the pit-head. Nothing unusual about that; our foreman, Lowry McWinnie comes back and says, "Lift the needles."

I must explain what this means.

The square pit shaft is halved in two-halves. To lift the needles lets you send our cage to the bottom which connects to the round pit. This could mean material could be sitting at ground level beside our cage that should have been sent down on nightshift on Saturday morning the 12th.

After a couple of minutes it rings again, this time when Lowrie comes back he looks different; he says nothing to us but he speaks to Wattie Reid. Then down comes the cage and goes straight through to the round pit; still no concern on our part, then she comes back up and stops at our level. It's full of men and Wattie Reid gets on at that time. Rickie Reid from Chryston comes into the pit bottom and I think he asks, "What is wrong?" Nobody knows except Lowrie. He says, "Something is wrong in the round pit," but he does not know what, but I remember Lowrie talking to some of the men on the cage; why did Wattie get on the cage I found out later.

After we had some tea and a sandwich the phone rings and Lowrie tells us all to get outside; we do so.

Then we hear the cage coming; it stops at us and what I see I will never forget. The manager, Bob Smillie, Alec Pettigrew, the under manager, also the safety officer and a lot of strangers who I did not recognise. The manager speaks to Lowrie and then they go on down.

Lowrie then goes to the phone and this time we can hear his conversation. He sent a message to Jimmy Lavery *(our trade union representative),* he is to come to the phone as soon as possible: it is urgent. After some time he contacts the pit bottom and Lowrie closes the door in the bothy and gives him a message. Time goes by and none of us afraid; we don't know anything, we are all guessing.

I then turned to move towards the square pit cage with all my own thoughts in my mind; thinking what was in front of us: a very hard day's work. You should not forget all the hutches from the Friday before had been sitting in the pit bottom since then and would be very hard to move. The hutches would be very heavy and we would have to pull and push to get them on to the cage; really hard work.

As we stepped onto the cage and then you look around, the man in front of you, the man to your left, and right of you they all become your family. That was an unwritten code of practice among the coalminer; everyone looked out for each other and would not stop to think about the dangers around themselves to help any person or persons if they were in any danger.

I left the coalmines and went in to construction industry. I can honestly say I have never met a work-mate like a coalminer, no never, you could trust him with your life.

The cage drops to the pit bottom and then begins the shift when I became a man that day in the square pit: the 18th Sept, 1959.

Can you imagine the scene? Here we are down a coalmine, the late Ricky Reid Chryston, Wattie Reid, *(no relation to Ricky)* then myself.

The three adult men where old Jock on the big haulage at the top of the big brae. Peter Toland *(he came from outside Muirhead)* somewhere on the empties in the tunnel at the top of the brae one of the coldest jobs in the pit bottom; the other being drawing empties from the back of the cage.

Lowrie McWinnie, pit bottomer, he also would load the cage with hutches and control everything to do with the pit bottom. Wattie was Lowrie's link with surface that's why he was sent up the pit when he was.

After some time past, a lamp beam came into view it was Jimmy Lavery, our Union rep. He spoke to Lowrie - their heads locked together. I remember all this as if it was yesterday it's so uncanny that all this has been away in the back of my memory for all these years and as I sit here in front of my computer it is all coming to the fore. I`m feeling so sad.

Jimmy ascended the pit: We were still not afraid: Why should we be? Remember we were six or seven boys and nine men. One, who knew of course, he knew he had his contact on the surface; maybe he was right to keep certain info to himself.

After another spell, dayshift miners started to drift into the pit bottom showing a lot of concern on their faces and when some spoke to Lowrie it started to sift through to us there was a fire in the round pit on the main road.

At this stage some of us took a walk around to the round pit shaft. This was a connection in that shaft; if anything happened in our shaft square pit, we could use that shaft to get to the surface. Not this time we couldn't.

It was just now acting like a chimney over a thousand-feet. Now, we had a problem, a very big one, we had only one escape route left that was down passed no: 4 main coal section and then through to wester Auchengeich - our sister pit, the Lumloch. This road had not been used for years and would have to be given a lot of looking at. Now some grave concern began to pass amongst all the men. Something we had not known all day until now and we had to address this situation. I, myself was still not afraid.

Then at about 2 o'clock word came through the phone. We had to get up the pit. I walked on to cage and stood there with the other fifteen men. As we rose to the surface you could start to feel the tension; it was all a wonder to me - three men missing.

The number was rising as we reached the surface: four then seven.

We left the cage and I walked out of the pit-head and looked at the crowd of people. Men, women with children in their arms; it was an amazing feeling. I can't explain how I felt as I walked to the lamp cabin.

When I came out the first person was my father. He asked me was I alright? I remember I answered him and said, I'm okay, dad. He turned and made his way back to Glasgow.

I then met my grandmother. She fainted into my arms and then was taken to the First Aid room. It was in the baths we were told that forty-seven men were trapped on the bogies in the main road of the round pit.

A fire had broken out near the fan. I remember a man from Dunlewy near Gweedore in Donegal was sitting next to me - Neil Roarty was his name. I can't repeat what he said to me, I forgot.

It was a crazy place nothing made sense to me. People coming and going. Ambulance sirenes going. Now I started to be afraid. Who was on them bogies? God, Who? I kept thinking to myself and you know whatß there was nothing I did not and cannot remember anymore until I was walking up to the top of the brae at Barr's farm and I turned and looked back at Auchengeich pit and saw a site I will never forget as long as I live.

The smoke from the round pit was getting blown towards Kirkintolloch area.

When I get to meet some of the people I worked with in the pit then I will write some more.

You see, what happens after Fri18th, Sept, 1959; we are all part of it together. Whole families were about to be destroyed forever by the events of this day.

May God Have Mercy On Their Souls
May They Rest In Peace.

Pat Doyle

In Words...

By Samual Barr

On 18 September, 1959, I was 29-years-old, and a roadsman at Auchengeich. I remember it was a pay day. I had started my morning shift in the square pit, travelling down in the bogies with Geordie Prentiss *(Prentice?)*.

We were waiting underground for the work to start and nothing was happening; there was no haulage or hutches.

I went to see if I could find out what was happening. I was told that there had been a fire in the round pit. There was a series of doors between the two shafts and I was taken through to see into the round pit.

All I could see was smoke in the shaft. Eventually we were allowed to return to the surface, where we finally learnt what had happened.

It was devastating. I remember that the Salvation Army were among the first on the scene, setting up a soup kitchen for the rescuers and those who were waiting for news.

It was two days before my first wedding anniversary. My wife, Nessie *(Agnes nee Florence)* was pregnant with our first child. We had tickets to the theatre for the following evening. We gave them away.

Samual Barr

In words...

By Samuel Green

I worked at Auchengeich pit. I was due to go down the shaft in the next cage when we were told that there was trouble down below. I knew my father, Thomas Green had gone down before me. We didn't know what was wrong and panic began to set in as the extent of what was going on below ground began to filter through.

My Father was brought up the mine on a stretcher by the rescue team but I didn't get to speak to him. I was told by a neighbour that my father was away in an ambulance to the Royal Infirmary in Glasgow.

My thought then was that I had to get there. Somebody ran me to the hospital; who it was I don't know.

By the time I got there my father had been attended to and was on his way back home. At that point a reporter approached me and introduced himself asking if I had anything to do with Auchengeich. I told him who I was and why I was there .

The reporter then offered me a run back home, which I accepted. I just wanted home to be with my family. On arriving in Glenboig the street was littered with reporters.

I took the man who had given me a run home into the house. It turned out he was from *The*

Sunday Mail and he managed to get rid of all the other reporters and photographers, who were doing their best to get pictures of my father.

I remember that one of the reporters even had a ladder up against the house trying to photograph inside. At this point we didn't know how many men were dead and how many had made it out. Obviously as time passed we found out that my father was the only one who made it out alive.

Samuel Green
Aged 26 at the time of the disaster.

In words...

By Thomas Skilling

On the 16th September 1959 my daughter, Carol was born and my wife and I were very happy not knowing of course what was about to happen two days later.

I was at work on the 18th when I was called to the office and told to go home as there was an emergency; as I was about to find out it was a disaster and that my father was involved.

There were a number of men trapped underground. For three days and nights the families of the men kept vigil, hoping and praying the men would be saved, but that was not to be. We were finally told the news that forty-seven men had died.

The Salvation Army – of which my father was a member – did their best to give comfort and help to all the families and also provided food and drinks which was a great help.

Those three days were the darkest days of my life. I had two brothers and two sisters and myself, being the oldest, I had to hold myself together for my mother and the rest of the family. My father was only fifty-three when he died and he was sadly missed by all of us and still is.

Thomas Skilling Son of William Skilling

In words...

By Tom Whiteside

I was almost four-years-old on 18 September, 1959. My father, Tom Stokes was a miner at Auchengeich. We lived in Gartferry Road, Bridgend, which was a few hundred yards from the pit.

I remember a man coming to our front door that morning and my mum rushed off with him. I remember seeing a trail of black smoke in the sky, and there were lots of people around, outside in the road and people hurrying up towards the pit.

At some point during the morning my brother and I were collected by our gran and we joined loads of other wives and daughters up at the pit-head. Everyone was just waiting but I had no idea what for. Being so young I just sat on the ground playing in a muddy puddle. Some people were giving out tea and I remember there was a Priest speaking to the women.

My uncle, John Rafferty, was one of the rescue team and I remember him coming over to speak to my mum and his big work boots were actually smoking, they were so hot.

I don't remember anyone crying or being hysterical, it was all weirdly calm. When the rescue operation was called off in the evening, we were already back at my gran's house.

I remember the funeral some time later, rows

of coffins going past the houses in Gartferry Road. Then we all moved away and life changed forever.

My father died aged thirty-two and left a wife and three sons, one of whom was just a tiny baby. Many years later my gran gave us newspaper cuttings of the day of the disaster and I can see myself sitting on the ground by the womens' feet.

Tom Whiteside

In words...

By Willie S Stewart

<u>Letter to Kirkintilloch Herald</u>

I have just received a copy of John Morrison's article *(11th Feb)* on the Auchengeich disaster and it has brought back memories of the terrible loss of life that happened on that Sept day.

In 1959 I was a young Scientific Tech Officer in the Coal Board working in the Dumbreck laboratory at Queenzieburn.

At about 7.10 am on that September morning my mother woke me and told me she had just heard on the radio that there had been an accident at a pit to the East of Glasgow.

My mind *(as I hurriedly dressed)* went into overdrive.

Was it Cardowan, Bedlay or the Lumloch? et cetera.

By the time I was dressed and ready to leave for work *(a matter of 10 mins),* there was another message on the radio, naming Auchengeich and saying that some men were trapped.

I left our house in Monkland Ave and my luck was in that day with the bus services as it was just before 8am I was in the lab.

Our Senior Scientist arrived on site at the same time and he told me to get to

Auchengeich.

The mobile laboratory had been despatched from Edinburgh and I was told to get operational as soon as it arrived. One of the van drivers took me to the site.

As we were approaching the entrance in front of us were two caravans; one was the mobile lab and the other the Salvation Army tea wagon. We quickly got the lab functioning. We were very familiar with the operation of this lab as many of us had spent three months the previous year monitoring an underground fire at Macharihanish. The responsibility of the mobile lab was to analyse underground air samples, checking for Methane, CO and CO_2.

Throughout the day we worked on the air samples, as people came into the lab we got various pieces of info on what had caused the disaster. We heard that it was a fan belt which had caught fire. Our Senior Scientist when he arrived on site immediately took samples of all belting held in the colliery store.

These samples would be tested for fireproofing qualities at the Area lab. Ten days after the disaster the samples were tested and one belt was found to be faulty, it was from the same batch that had been used on the faulty fan.

On Saturday 19th a visitor was brought into the lab and we were asked to explain to him about our work. He was a young priest called Tom and it was many years later when I realised that our visitor was now Archbishop Tom Winning.

After we finished talking I took him across to

pit-head where he met other officials. I knew several of the men who lost their lives that day; having gone to school with their families. One man I knew very well was Frank Fisher who was the First Aid Instructor in 1st Kirk. BB Coy - I was the BB Capt and I am sure there are still men in Kirk who will still be using the First Aid techniques taught to them by Frank fifty-years ago.

Fifty years ago Scotland and the mining community lost a lot of good men in this disaster.

Notes

1. Frank Fisher was the First Aid instructor in the 1st Kirkintilloch Boys' Brigade Coy. I was the Captain of the Company. He was well-respected by the boys and I am sure that there are some men in Kirkintilloch today who are still using the advice given to them as boys in the late 1950s. Frank would occasionally turn up at our Bible class and he would quietly ask me before the service what were the hymns that we would be singing and I also knew why he was asking the question. Frank's favourite hymn was *'Eternal Father Strong to Save',* and it was always sung when he was present. To this day I always think of it as, 'Frank's hymn'.

2. On Saturday morning 19th we were working in the mobile laboratory when our Area Chief Scientist brought in a Priest and introduced him to the staff on duty. We explained to him what our role was in the

accident and sat for a time talking to him about the situation. The Chief Scientist asked me to take the Father across to the pit head; the lab was a distance away from main area. We walked across the rail lines and talked about the situation and he spoke to several different groups of people on our way across to the pit. It was many years afterwards that I remembered his name - Father Tom Winning. Little did he or I know that he would eventually be the most important Roman Catholic Priest in Scotland.

3. Our Deputy Chief Scientist first action as soon as he arrived on site was to put an embargo on the movement of any belt materials in the colliery store. He then proceeded to take samples of all rolls of belt held in the store. We kept the samples in the mobile lab and logged them into our record book. It would be another two weeks before we were able to test all the samples for fireproofing back at the Area Laboratory at Dumbreck Colliery. We tested all the samples and only one failed and when we checked back our records the same roll had failed about a month before. It was fan belt material and although no-one said it, I am pretty certain it was from the same batch as the belt on the underground fan which had caused the accident.

4. As Scientific Tech Officers our job was to analyse air samples from the pit. We checked for Methane, Carbon Dioxide, Oxygen and

Carbon Monoxide. Many of our team had spent many hours in the mobile laboratory as there had been a fire in Macharahanish Mine at Campbeltown in 1958, indeed the fire started on 18th Sept - one year earlier than the Auchengeich accident. We were very familiar with the operations of the laboratory and we did not have any problems in handling this accident.

The only thing that worried us was that we knew that several of our group were going back to university and we were worried about setting reasonable rota lists. As it happened this was not a problem although I personally was on duty for 50-hours and it was 53-hours before I returned home to Kirkintilloch; having left the house at 7.30am on the Friday.

5. On Sunday 4th Oct 1959 it was Youth Sunday in our church, St David's Ledgate, Kirkintilloch and the B.B Coy were on parade. The service had just started when one of the elders came into Church and whispered a message to me. I was required to contact my Area Chief Scientist.

In the Church entrance was our laboratory driver who asked me to ring Mr Hindmarch *(before the days of mobile phones)*. We found a public telephone box and I made a reversed charges call to the Chief. He instructed me to go to Auchengeich Colliery and investigate a possible underground heating. The driver, (I can't remember his name - Wilson or Duffy?) had collected my kit from the laboratory and we drove to Auchengeich where I met an under manager who briefed me on the situation. On his morning inspection he thought that there was a heating on the main roadway. We went underground to inspect the site and try to determine the size of the problem. I did a Carbon Monoxide check using MSA Draeger tubes and this gave a positive reading. We then took further air samples and returned to the surface where I analysed the samples and found them to be high in CO_2 and CO, very low in methane. The view taken by the under manager was that gas was leaking from behind the stopping which had been put in place after the disaster. The decision was that this leak would be sealed. Unfortunately I don't know when the sealing took place.

Willie S Stewart

**Remembering the miners
whose lamps still shine brightly**

Forty-seven fine men...

Aaron Price
We will never see his likes again

Remembering...

Aaron
Price

In Loving Memory

Alexander Morrison Beattie
His lamp still shines

Remembering...

Alexander
Morrison
Beattie

In Loving Memory

Alexander Sharp

Never shall he be forgotten

Remembering...

Alexander
Sharp

In Loving Memory

Alexander Todd Lang
His light brightly shines

Remembering...

**Alexander
Todd
Lang**

In Loving Memory

Andrew Crombie

True legend of the mines

Remembering...

Andrew
Crombie

In Loving Memory

Andrew Docherty

Brave of the mines, love of the pit

Remembering...

Andrew
Docherty

In Loving Memory

Andrew McKenna

Lost but always here

Remembering...

Andrew
McKenna

In Loving Memory

Denis McElhaney
A true symbol of bravery

Remembering...

Denis
McElhaney

In Loving Memory

Donald Cameron Weir

His lamp shall forever light the way

Remembering...

Donald
Cameron
Weir

In Loving Memory

Edward Henery

His energy unbreakable, his light eternal

Remembering...

Edward
Henery

In Loving Memory

Francis Broadley

A gift sent from above

Remembering...

Francis
Broadley

In Loving Memory

Francis J Fisher

Broken hearts mended only by your love

Remembering...

Francis J. Fisher

In Loving Memory

Francis Kiernan

Forever in our hearts

Remembering...

Francis Kiernan

In Loving Memory

George Jackson
An eternal cradle, touched by the wind

Remembering...

George
Jackson

In Loving Memory

George Thomas
T. McEwan
Heaven is a richer place for your presence

Remembering...

George
Thomas T.
McEwan

In Loving Memory

George Wilkie McIntosh

The bridge to our hearts, the river to our souls

Remembering...

George
Wilkie
McIntosh

In Loving Memory

Gerald J Martin

The flowers in our park, the light in our way

Remembering...

Gerald J. Martin

In Loving Memory

Henry Clayton

Until we meet again

Remembering...

Henry
Clayton

In Loving Memory

James Devine
When will we see his likes again?

Remembering...

James
Devine

In Loving Memory

James Harvey
In our hearts we remember, fondly

Remembering...

James
Harvey

In Loving Memory

James McPhee
A shining star in the deep dark sky

Remembering...

James
McPhee

In Loving Memory

James Nimmo

In our darkest hours you shine the light

Remembering...

James
Nimmo

In Loving Memory

John Duffy

Never far from our thoughts

Remembering...

John
Duffy

In Loving Memory

John M Stark

You keep us strong, you keep us safe

Remembering...

John M.
Stark

In Loving Memory

John McAuley

You lead the way when we are lost

Remembering...

John
McAuley

In Loving Memory

John Muir

*In each of our prayers, always in our
thoughts*

Remembering...

John
Muir

In Loving Memory

John Mulholland Snr

Our forever guide and comfort

Remembering...

John
Mulholland
Snr

In Loving Memory

John Shevlin
Never a day goes by, thinking of you always

Remembering...

John
Shevlin

In Loving Memory

Joseph McDonald

You built the stones that we walk upon

Remembering...

Joseph
McDonald

In Loving Memory

Martin Fleming
Touched by an angel

Remembering...

Martin
Fleming

In Loving Memory

Matthew McIwain Cannon
One of a kind, greatly missed

Remembering...

Matthew
McIwain
Cannon

In Loving Memory

Michael Fleming

Bringing us light every day

Remembering...

Michael
Fleming

In Loving Memory

Patrick Harvey

True hero, true gentleman

Remembering...

Patrick
Harvey

In Loving Memory

Peter Kelly

*Built the rock in our family and the bond
in our community*

Remembering...

Peter
Kelly

In Loving Memory

Peter McMillan

Brave soldier of the dark, true guidance to the light

Remembering...

Peter
McMillan

In Loving Memory

Richard Hamilton

Watching over us, comforting us and always there

Remembering...

Richard
Hamilton

In Loving Memory

Robert Conn

Paving our way in moments of uncertainty

Remembering...

Robert
Conn

In Loving Memory

Robert McCoid

Never shall we forget, always in our hearts

Remembering...

Robert
McCoid

In Loving Memory

Robert Price

In our hearts, minds and prayers - every day

Remembering...

Robert
Price

In Loving Memory

Thomas Bone

A reflection in the day, a safe warm blanket in the night

Remembering...

Thomas
Bone

In Loving Memory

Thomas Stokes

An honourable presence in heaven

Remembering...

Thomas
Stokes

In Loving Memory

Walter Clark
Never far away from us, always close by

Remembering...

Walter
Clark

In Loving Memory

William Brynes
Walking by us side-by-side, each step of the way

Remembering...

William
Brynes

In Loving Memory

William Lafferty

At peace, knowing you are here, safe and guiding us

Remembering...

**William
Lafferty**

In Loving Memory

William Leishman

With angels you fly, with us you live each day in our hearts and thoughts

Remembering...

William
Leishman

In Loving Memory

William Meechan

*Everywhere we go, you are there for us
and with us*

Remembering...

William
Meechan

In Loving Memory

William Skilling

You are the fire that keeps us warm, you are the light that guides our way

Remembering...

William
Skilling

In Loving Memory

50th Memorial Service

The 50 th anniversary on Sept 18th , 2009 was marked by a wonderful service, packed house surrounded by a sincere and beautiful setting. The scene could have been fitting for a magnificent film but this was no entertainment. This was a tribute of the highest order possible where around six-hundred people congregated to pay their respects to the brave men who gave their lives that day so that decent, honest, hard-working folks could enjoy a warm home. Forty-seven brave miners set off to work that day and never did return.

Fifty years on the hurt, the loss and the pain still etched on humble faces like they had just rested their loved ones to peace a day or so before. Fifty years on and the old saying of, 'Time is a great healer,' simply did not apply. The comfort, if you could call it so, was the floral tributes, the speeches, the respect shown by the community and beyond and many came from distant shores to join hearts and remember one of Scotland's worst disasters.

Old men weeped openly, old women reached for their soft tissues and didn't care if the wiping of their tears smudged their carefully-applied make-up; this was a day to remember and a day not to forget. Young people joined in gracefully, mingling in with the elder community members like they were all part of the family. Well, they are part of the family and like all those years ago when communities were said to be tighter and more protective of their young; the new generation blended in under the wings of their elderly protectors – as they always did during the days of old.

It was a beautiful moment to remember. It was a wonderful day and blessed memorial: fitting only for forty-seven princes and kings.

One image stood out amongst the solemn crowd; the bronze statue, a unique and aura-filled presence that oozed with every detail, curve and form posed in humble-like stance but had the grace and stature of a God. The wonderful statue, by John McKenna, was a marvellous icon and you could see the work put into the statue was as precise as it was real-life like. The statue topped many a tribute given to the memorial; and you could not help but admire how hard working in the mines really was – and still is – when you see the strength, posture and it even had the sweat of labour finish to a great body of works. What stood out was the statue's head; it was lowered as if to express his own respects. In all, it was a hugely magnificent tribute and a world-class piece of art.

Rt. Hon. Alex Salmond M.S.P. attended the memorial service as were the media and many honourable people from all walks including top-level politicians. It was the families of the forty-seven *lost-but-not-forgotten* brave men who stood proudly side-by-side and arm-in-arm as each poignant message was read. The beautiful garden, dedicated to the forty-seven miners, displayed an assortment of colours that added light and hope to the day.

The day was marked across the globe in many different time zones. Relatives and friends from all over the world paid their respects in their own private way. Emails came flooding in to the Black Gold project where many people said they were sorry they could not attend the memorial service but will be thinking of that fateful day back in Sept 18th , 1959, and will be remembering their friends and families.

The day was perfectly-laid out in terms of organization, the people who worked constantly behind-the-scenes, and the mass of people who attended in their Sunday best attire. It was the best memorial service anyone involved could have wished for and the brave forty-seven men would be proud of the occasion.

It is difficult to comprehend how fifty years can go by so quickly for some and so slowly for others. Disasters all over the world are marked with anniversaries and as time moves on and yes, family members do get older, for those family members it must seem as if time has not moved on, or not moved on that much. The loss of a loved one and the pain never really eases.

Any miner will tell you that the loss of a miner is not just a fellow worker; it is the loss of a great friend. It is the loss of a brother.

A Rescue Miner's Daughter
...Patricia's Story

My father, Eric Savage, was only in the service for about six months when the Auchengeich Colliery disaster struck. He was a fledgling brigadesman, aged 23-year-old.

We lived in the Mines Rescue houses in Coatbridge. The single quarters were above the station but everyone got together in the family quarters where a range of activities would unfold like listening to the football on the radio, have a blether, participating in the occasional wee dram or two and all the Mines Rescue brigadesmen and their families lived in each others' houses like it was the most natural thing on earth. A close-knit community. Being a family, we lived in the so-named married quarters.

The housing complex was almost like a fire station with its on-site equipment, vehicles which were well-equipped, and workshop. It was all very, regimented, secure and extremely well-organized. The recovery equipment was of the highest standard imaginable and the First-Aid skills were as close as you can get to that of a nurse's treatment. The 'big bell' was only ever a ring away and you never knew if it was a call out to a fire incident, gas, poison or electrical but the rescuers were always at the ready. Taking the nature of the dangers of mining it was no surprise that the rescue people were more like first responders with skills of a fire fighter and a paramedic all rolled into one.

I recall my Dad sitting a number of exams during my childhood. The knowledge and skill required to be a Mines Rescue brigadesman had to be of the highest standard. You really had to be up-to-speed on subjects like: vulnerability levels, admission points of gases and geological structure. Education was the key to progression. Fitness levels paramount, First-Aid competitions to keep your skills fresh and second nature.

Fortunately I was born 18-months after the terrible Auchengeich disaster but that awful day in Sept 18th , 1959, will always be with my Dad. A tragedy like that never leaves you.

 I was born and grew up amongst the mining community, more typically the Mines Rescue community and many others in my position will remember what it was like growing up in such a community. There is something really special about being part of the 'mining family' and the closeness we all had for each other and how we lived is testament to how unique being part of that sort of community really is. They are so close that a disaster – however bad enough in any circumstance – seems to hit miners really, really badly. It is one big family, the generations working alongside each other, so one loss is bad enough but losing forty-seven from that big family is absolutely horrific. Words cannot possibly convey the utter devastation felt by the people of that community.

I had a wonderful childhood and being part of the Mines Rescue community made that childhood special for me. Being part of that Mines Rescue community, also meant the possibilities were always close at hand for moving to another station. My Dad served four years at the station in Cowdenbeath. Cowdenbeath was a somewhat smaller station but we had a wee back garden and a semi-detached house rather than a terraced house. Surrounded by people who cared about you and the mischief you sometimes got up to! Nothing went un-noticed .

At Coatbridge Station the dog racing track faced our house *(now the police station),* and I had great times watching the dogs racing from the comfort of my own bedroom window. I was so used to it and gathered enough knowledge that I actually became a good tipster, providing valuable entertainment for us kids and betting the odd sweetie on the outcome.

The scrap yard near us might be a scrap yard to others but to the kids it was paradise. We used it as a playground. We would make dens out of the old abandoned cars and have a picnic with a packet of Cream Crackers and a bottle of lemonade. Never mind rusty metal and jaggy bits from broken cars sticking out; we played there! Reliving scenes from the films we'd seen at the ABC picture house on a Saturday morning. So much for child safety back then but it was a fun place to be; it certainly gave us a very creative and enjoyable environment to grow up in.

As kids we got up to all sorts of mischief and when you do that you run the risks and the wrath of the consequences but when a crab apple tree is full to the brim, just waiting on its contents to be plucked, you cannot stop that invite when you are young, adventurous and if you were like me – a tomboy – then that apple tree was fair game. It may resemble a scene from an Enid Blyton book with the adventurous surroundings and the hunt for apples but my Dad soon put a stop to that when he saw me hanging off a tree, opposite his office window, that just so happened to be dangling over the railway line and would you believe the irony if it all; whilst hanging off the end of that tree, hovering above the railway line, a coal train passed by underneath me. That was to be the last time I would be going for apples on trees. I got my back side skelped all the way home and very early to bed!

Indeed, it was a magical time and place to grow up in. We were no different from any other kids but we did live in an inside outside world where we lived in our close quarters but still had the freedom to go outside and do things like fishing. Well, all I ever caught was a case of the jaundice and if I was lucky some wee baggy minnows.

I also remember the bread strike, in the early 1970s, buying the wrong flour for my Mum, who was trying her hand at baking her own bread. We all learned how to queue and share the vital things. Well, we were all part of one big family and lived and breathed in each others' homes and lives. The big kids looked after the wee kids and the mums looked after us all.

The seasons growing up in the mining community were extra special. I remember with great fondness our Halloween nights and of course, Christmas. Treacle scones *(made with black treacle)* were a delight and the mothers used to make their own sweets *(mostly cinder toffee)*. Kids dressed up and doing a wee turn to gain some sweets or a sixpence. Bonfire nights shortly afterwards were great occasions. I can still see the pile of old and unwanted furniture and the crowds would gather to bake their potatoes and watch the fireworks, our mums and dads had clubbed together to buy.

Christmas was another level up. If you thought Halloween was great and bonfire night then Christmas topped it for us kids. The families would gather to make Christmas that extra bit special. We would have the party in the empty Station house, now covered in tinsel and streamers, and a huge Christmas tree twinkling in the corner; our hearts were jumping with the excitement of it all. Great long tables weighed down by sandwiches and tooth-rotting cakes and sweets. Dancing the *Dashing White Sergeant* or a waltz, which I would dance standing on my Dad's toes. We danced the lot, the *Gay Gordons,* the *Oki Koki,* you name it. The adults would do a party piece, sing a song or tell a joke. The highlight for us kids was when Santa arrived with our presents. At the end about fifty people would all gather and sing *Auld Lang Syne* and the huge net filled with balloons that stretched across the ceiling would release its quarry and thirty kids would dash around trying to burst them all. The closeness felt in those times tells you a lot of how the Mines Rescue people really lived. Our Dads did something unusual and difficult for a living but we were cocooned from the nature of their work and they made the time they spent with us so tangibly memorable.

For holidays we didn't board flights; we took a long car journey and visited places like Loch Lomond. Car piled with belongings, a team of kids, a camping gas fire to keep us warm when we got there and the journey was made all that much smoother with a packet of plain crisps and a packet of Spangles.

Those were the moments that stand out for me. How the adults in the community did everything to make our childhoods that bit special and even when my Dad got a call out there must have been some kind of code word in our house because as soon as that call came in for a possible rescue assignment we were all sitting in front of the TV with a wee glass of milk. No fuss. Now, as an adult, I realise it was more to protect us from the reality of how dangerous things could turn out in the mining business. Supporting each other through the most harrowing times and celebrating the best of times.

At the age of forty-five you had to step down from your underground duties. My Dad's words, on his retirement, will always stay with me and hopefully let others know what his time in the Mines Rescue meant to him, when he said: "It was a privilege to service the community that brought me up. To give something back to the men underground who saw something in me and made me apply for a job with the Mines Rescue. I owe it all to them."

Auchengeich Colliery, Lanarkshire.
18th September 1959
'Black Smoke over the Cornfields'
A Mining Disaster

Background

The Colliery

The year was 1959; and the month was September. It had been an exceptional summer, one of the warmest and longest of the 20th century in Britain. This Indian summer had lasted well into the latter part of September. The rolling fields of this part of North Lanarkshire were producing a rich harvest of cereals, which were processed at two separate water powered grain mills situated on the River Luggie and one of its tributaries. There was also a rich harvest to be won from the coal seams below these fields. This coal was suitable for processing to produce a valuable metallurgical coke to feed the iron and steel works of Lanarkshire, which in turn fed the famous shipbuilding yards on the River Clyde at Glasgow. Auchengeich Colliery was situated at Chryston in the County of Lanark, some seven miles north east of Glasgow.

This mine was gassy and large percentages of methane were normally released during coal production in its coals seams. It had two shafts, each reaching the No2 (Round Pit) workings where the accident, to be described later, occurred at a depth of 360 yards. This shaft was for ventilation purposes and referred to as the upcast shaft, from which the air was returned to the surface after its circulation in the mine. The No 1 (Square Pit), the downcast shaft, was where the air travelled into the mine workings. This shaft had two hinged gratings, known as "needles", fitted at a depth of about 150 yards, where there was an inset for the No 1 Pit workings in the Meiklehill Wee Seam, below which cages were not normally wound.

At the time of the accident, some 830 were employed at the mine producing about 730 tons daily. In the No 2 Pit Workings, there were 340 men, about 140 on each of the day and afternoon shifts and 60 on the night shift; the daily output was about 380 ton from the Meiklehill Main Coal and the Kilsyth Coking Coal Seam. The night shift ascended between 6.00 and 6.30 am and the day shift men were lowered between 6.30 and 7.00 am.

No 2 Pit Workings

There were two main roads running generally parallel in a southerly direction to the workings in the Main Coal and Coking Coal Seams. The intake airway was used for the haulage of coal tubs by endless rope and the first 925 yards of the return airway for a man-riding haulage system. As well as the connections near the pit bottom, there was a crosscut with air separation doors, commonly known as Johnston's Crosscut, some 1,125 yards inbye. Two more crosscuts, each with doors, were provided farther inbye in the vicinity of No 6 Bench, the branch haulage road leading to the Coking Coal Sections. The return airway from these sections crossed the intake airway by an overcast and then joined the main return airway between these connecting crosscuts. The booster fan, at which the fire which caused the disaster occurred, was in the return airway, a little further outbye.

The System of Ventilation

The Intake air ventilating the No 2 Pit Working split at No 6 Bench to provide separate intakes to the Main Coal and Coking Coal sections. The return air from these sections came together at No 5 Bench and then passed through the booster fan situated about 40 yards outbye, at a point some 570 yards from Johnston's Crosscut and about a mile from the pit bottom. The exhausting fan at the surface was electrically driven and produced 160,000 cubic feet per minute, at 5.5 inches watergauge. A standby fan had a similar capacity.

The Booster Fan

The booster fan was of a double inlet forward–bladed centrifugal type, with a 45 inch diameter rotor driven by a flat belt. The manufacturer's catalogue it indicates that this type of size of fan is provided for 64 blades.

The fan was not fitted with an evasee. The rotor shaft was carried on two white metal bearings, oil ring lubricated and each with a capacity of about six pints of oil. The cambered, or "crowned", fan pulley was 22½ inches in diameter, 12 inches wide and overhung the bearing. It was driven at about 540 revolutions per minute by a 100 horsepower, flameproof slip-ring induction motor, running at 730 revolutions per minute. The power supply was three-phase, 50 cycle alternating current at 440 volts. The motor pulley, also "crowned", was 16¾ inches in diameter and 15 inches wide; the pulley centres were 15 feet apart. The fan was fenced on the near side with one inch aperture steel wire mesh, supported on an angle iron frame, secured to a sidewall of the fan house. A timber covering, or "catwalk", made from nine inch by two inch batten, was placed over the belt to facilitate access to the nearest fan bearing.

The transmission belt was seven-ply and twelve inches wide. It was of a type known as balata belting, made of a folded high tensile cotton duck and balata gum, neither of which was fire-resistant. In the absence of slip, the belt speed would have been about 3,200 feet per minute.

The fan was situated in a fan house in the main return airway, with the outlet casing mounted in a brick wall built across this roadway and with brick wall fairing to smooth the airflow into the two inlets of the fan. The motor was mounted on three slide rails, which afforded a travel of about seven inches for tensioning the belt. The circuit breaker and rotor starter for the motor were in the crosscut adjacent to the motor. A u-tube watergauge and an automatic indicator of the water gauge, situated near a haulage house towards the intake end of this crosscut, indicated and recorded the ventilation pressure between the intake and return airways. Three wooden doors in a by-pass roadway were designed to open automatically by a change in ventilation pressure in the event of a fan stoppage.

The sides of the road inbye of the fan to its junction with the by-pass roadway were mainly of brickwork and the roof was supported by steel girders. Looking outbye from the fan, on the left-hand side of the road was a brick wall to the wire mesh safety fence. On the right-hand side of the road, for a distance of about 12 feet from the fan, there was a brick wall six feet high, on which some short wooden props were set to support roof girders; for the remainder of the distance to the safety fence, upright girders were used to support the roof girders. The girders on the roof and sides were lagged with wood; none of the wood had been fire-proofed.

The Man-Riding Haulage

The man-riding haulage was an endless under-rope (wire) system of modern design, in which each car or bogie was attached to the wire rope by an integral screw clip. The train comprised four bogies, each seating 12 men in three compartments having seats for four, two facing each way. The electrically driven engine, housed in the return airway, was provided with protection against over-running at each end of the haulage and against excessive speed; the position of the bogies through the journey was shown on an indicator and, at each end, by a warning stop-light.

Fire-Fighting Equipment

The positions of the water mains valves, hydrants and other fire-fighting equipment in the vicinity of the booster fan in the return road, as described by witnesses, are recorded on the plan. Fire hoses were kept only on the surface.

Colliery Telephones

The main telephone switchboard was in the lamp room on the surface, with lines to telephones in the colliery office, the engineers' surface workshop, the winding engine rooms, the pit-head and down the shafts. The line from the surface to the upcast pit bottom terminated at a small switchboard in a pumphouse connected to instruments at Johnston's Crosscut, No 6 Bench and at various other points farther inbye. Conversations between any two points could be overheard on instruments situated elsewhere. There was no telephone communication on the man-riding haulage system.

Events on the day of the fire

Timing

It became apparent quite early in the Inquiry into the disaster, that there was a period of an hour or so during which every minute was potentially significant in considering whether or not, once the fire had started, anything could have been done to avert the loss of life. The Commissioner of the Inquiry was favourably impressed by the way in which witnesses, without exception, gave their evidence, but it is nevertheless necessary to keep constantly in mind their difficulty in the timing of events. Very few of the witnesses carried watches, and it can be by no means certain that those which were carried were accurate. In these circumstances, it is surprising that the estimated times tie in as well as they do; but it might nevertheless be misleading to place too much reliance upon any one time quoted.

Appearance of Haze

At about 6.25 am on Friday 18th September 1959, after most of the night shift had gone up to the pit top and before the dayshift had gone underground, A Paton, the night shift engineman in charge of the man-riding haulage, was waiting in his engine house near the upcast pit bottom to be relieved by T Campbell, when he noticed a slight haze and a very slight smell of something burning. He was not perturbed, but went to the pit bottom and met the first cage of the day-shift men just after 6.30 am. One of these was J H Dickson, the day shift assistant overman; Paton drew Dickson's attention to the haze and smell. Dickson was suffering from a cold and could not smell anything, but he sensed signs of a "kind of heat" in the air. He decided to investigate inbye and told an oncost (day-wage) worker to inform R Boyd, the day shift overman, when he came down the pit. Paton went back to his engine house and ran the first train down to the man-riding haulage road. Many of the men on this train gave evidence about the haze in the pit bottom; although some sensed that all might not be well inbye, none seemed to have been in any way alarmed. The train left at 6.40 am, or perhaps a minute or two before, with Dickson and about seventeen others. The normal journey time was about eight minutes, so it would have arrived at the inbye two or three minutes after 6.45 am. There was not an appointed guard on this train, but it was signalled back to the pit bottom.

Some of the men on the train, including Dickson, said that the haze at the inbye terminus of the man-riding haulage was, perhaps, very slightly thicker than at the pit bottom, but they were still not alarmed. It was the usual practise for some of them to continue to travel along the return airway towards their working places. On this occasion, Dickson decided as a precaution that all the men should accompany him through Johnston's Crosscut into the intake airway, and he passed back instructions to that effect. The men followed him into the intake airway, then inbye to the crosscut nearest the Booster Fan, arriving there at about 7.00 am.

Discovery of the Fire

Dickson went alone through the doors at the back of No 5 haulage engine into the fan house and there found flames rising from the fan drive belt, which had apparently burned through and was lying on the floor with the ends about three feet from the motor pulley. He said that the belt was around the fan pulley and that flames from the belt were being drawn into the fan casing. The Commissioner, as recorded in more detail later, said that others who followed Dickson into the fan house saw the fan casing and oil around the bearings burning, and going through the by-pass doors saw flame coming from the fan outlet into the return airway at, or shortly after, 7.05 am.

At the Shaft Bottoms

Meanwhile, the day shift overman, Boyd, who was down the pit by about 6.50 am, had received Dickson's message and had gone to the main switches near the downcast shaft, with the intention of switching off all the electric current going to the inbye districts. He was, however, uncertain about the switching arrangements, so he told D Kirkpatrick, a pump maintenance man, who was conversant with the switchgear, to cut off the electrical current. To make sure that this would not affect the No 1 Pit workings, Boyd decided to telephone to an electrician on the surface. While he was trying to do this, he overheard Dickson on the telephone saying that the fan was ablaze. The time would, according to his movements, have been just after 7.00 am. In the meantime, J Thornton, an electrician, had reached the pit bottom and Boyd sent him to the main switches to check that the electric current was off the fan. The electrician went to the switches and then telephoned Dickson, asking him to cut off the electricity to the fan motor.

After he had been to the switches, but before he went to the telephone, Boyd had told an oncost worker to give a message to Campbell in the main haulage engine house. The message was overheard by a conveyor beltman, but the precise form it took is a little uncertain; it seems to the effect that no one was to be let down the man-riding haulage until further instructions were given. Boyd said, in evidence, that he intended that any men in the haulage were to be withdrawn, but his words possibly did not convey that meaning. He then walked inbye down the intake airway; on the way he met a brusher who had been sent by Dickson to Johnston's Crosscut to stop any men going into the return airway beyond that point. Boyd felt sure he had stopped all men coming in, so he took the brusher in with him to the fan, which he reached shortly after 7.30 am.

Paton, on receiving the appropriate signal started to haul the empty train outbye, but was then, at about 6.50 am, relieved by Campbell. Paton walked to the cage and went up the shaft. On the surface he told D McKinnon, the Chief Engineer, and A Pettigrew, the Under-Manager, that there was a haze in the return airway. Pettigrew suspected that the haze was being caused by the fan drive belt, which he knew had been giving trouble during the night shift. He went to the lamp room and telephoned a warning to the overman in No.1 Pit, telling him that the booster fan might not be working. He had just finished this telephone conversation when a call from Dickson was received in the lamp room. McKinnon and Pettigrew, after informing the manager, went down the upcast shaft, No 2 pit, at about 7.10 am, taking with them a new fan belt, which McKinnon had earlier sent to the pit-head. It evidently did not occur to them that there was imminent danger to men in the No 2 pit, and their sole purpose in mind was to put the fire out and restart the fan. At the bottom of the upcast shaft, Pettigrew and McKinnon encountered fairly dense smoke. Pettigrew saw a number of the day shift men from the return airway. He went down the intake airway with McKinnon and D McAuley, a mechanic.

Second Train Journey

The first train returned to the outbye terminus probably a little after 6.55 am. Forty-eight men then boarded the bogies to go inbye. This train, according to the engineman, left at 7.00am, or perhaps a few minutes before. The recollection of T Green, the sole survivor of the men on this train, was that the haze thickened very slightly during the journey to the inbye terminus. With a journey time of eight minutes, the train would have arrived inbye at, or shortly after, 7.05 am. None of the men left the vicinity of the inbye terminus, however, because the arrival of the train there more or less coincided with a thick blanket of smoke which came along the return airway towards them. By common consent, they decided that it was impossible to proceed inbye and they re-boarded the bogies. Campbell received a signal to haul outbye and started to do so; he then received a signal to stop and start the train three times in quick succession; but when the train eventually got underway it did not stop again until it was near the outbye terminus. The sequence of signal is borne out in the evidence of men who were near the engine house. Green, on the other hand, only recollected the train stopping once after it left the inbye terminus; this was at the top of the 1 in 5 gradient, when the train was stopped so that one of the passengers, who was slumping off the bogie, could be pulled back into his seat. This was done and the train signalled away again after a delay, which Green put at a few moments. The smoke, according to Green, was very thick indeed; he covered his mouth and nose as best he could with his jacket. He was at the outbye end of the train and when it stopped before it reached the terminus near the engine house, he got off and stumbled outbye, until he was overcome, just after passing the gate at the outbye end of the man-riding haulage road. As described later, he was rescued. None of the other forty-seven men on the bogies escaped from the return roadway. Indeed, as they were found later, it was apparent that forty-three of them had been overcome as they sat on the bogies; one appeared to have fallen from the train about 300 yards inbye; only three seemed to have been able to attempt an escape, and they succumbed quite close to the train.

Earlier, as the ingoing train was nearing the inbye terminus, Campbell had received Boyd's message about not letting any more men down the haulage. He construed the message as meaning that his authorised guard, and any men who remained on the bogies, were to be withdrawn. He was not unduly worried at the time, however, because the haze at the engine house had not appreciably worsened since he had taken over from Paton. When he received the first signal to bring the bogies outbye, Campbell assumed that only the guard was on board; the subsequent signals to stop and start, however, led him to think that something had gone wrong. The train was about half way out when the haze at the engine house turned to thick smoke, and he could not see his train position indicator. Conditions became even worse, and Campbell, feeling he could not stay there any longer, was faced with the difficult decision whether or not to stop the train. He was still unaware how many men were aboard the bogies and, as conditions became impossible for him, it passed through his mind that he might leave the engine house without stopping the engine. The train would have continued to the outbye terminus, where the engine would have cut out automatically. He was slowing the engine down when he heard a voice, and he then decided to stop the bogies for fear of running down any men who might be trying to escape on foot. He brought the train to rest about 100 yards from the terminus. By this time, probably just about 7.15 am, Campbell himself was almost overcome, but he was able to make his way out through the separation doors near the main coal haulage engine to the intake airway, whence he later rode in the downcast shaft to the surface.

Rescues at the Shaft Bottom

A number of men were waiting near the outbye terminus for a third train to take them inbye, when the haze thickened to smoke. They went into the fresh air, which was leaking through the separation doors in a connection a short distance outbye; but, whilst waiting there, they heard sounds indicating that someone was moving. Some of them went back into the smoke and found Green by groping in an atmosphere with visibility at zero. They took him to the upcast shaft bottom, whence he was taken to the surface. G Brown, the onsetter at the upcast shaft bottom, was then also overcome and taken into the intake air, then up the downcast shaft. Those who rescued Green and Brown, some of whom took part in both rescues, acted with undoubted courage and the Commissioner was glad to associate himself with the tributes paid to them by representatives of all parties at the Inquiry. Among those men who performed these rescues were A Coyle, T Alpin, P McKeown, J McConnachie and Edward Savage.

At the Fire

After discovering the belt ablaze, Dickson stopped the motor, hurried to No 5 haulage house, a distance of about 50 yards, and picked up a fire extinguisher. He took it to the fire, but found it would not work. He therefore instructed A Cunningham, a deputy, and others who had followed to the fan, to try to smother the fire with sand and stone dust, while he went to the telephone. He telephoned the surface from the No 6 Bench, about 100 yards from the fan, and asked for extinguishers to be sent down. As officials had been instructed by the manager to notify No 1 pit working if the fan stopped, Dickson gave a warning that it was not working. He collected another fire extinguisher from No. 6 Transformer House but found, on his return to the fan, this extinguisher also would not work. He did not look for more extinguishers, but returned to the telephone at No. 6 Bench and, probably a few moments after 7.05 am, made the call in which he asked for extinguishers and hoses. He said that, when making one of his telephone calls, he had to wait a minute or two before the pumpman, who attended to the switchboard at the shaft bottom, put his call through to the surface. Dickson went to the No. 5 Bench to prepare the hydrant there for the fire hoses, but he found the water range blanked off. There was a hydrant some 300 yards away in No 6 roadway. He thought this too distant and decided to take the hydrant and fix it on the water range at No. 5 Bench. He was assisted in this by others and the hydrant was ready when the hoses arrived from the surface some time later. At about 7.15 am he made a further telephone call to the surface; he spoke to D Gray, a general duties man, in the lamp room and asked for the Rescue Brigade to be summoned. Up to this time Dickson had seen only the fire inside the fan house.

Two deputies, M Lynch and J Roe, had walked down the return airway after the first train had left. They had come through Johnston's Crosscut to the intake airway and arrived at the fan shortly after Dickson. They and others had seen the fan casing and oil from the bearings burning at 7.05 am, or perhaps a little later. Roe helped Lynch to put stone dust on the fire for a very short time then, probably just after 7.05 am, went through the three by-pass doors. Lynch, who had local fire service experience, tested the extinguishers that had failed when Dickson tried to use them and he, too, found them unworkable. He then followed Roe through the doors. Both men saw flames coming from the fan outlet and striking the roof and the right-hand side of the road between the fan and safety fence. F Macdonald, a brusher, said that at 7.15 am the belt had been reduced to ash. The fan casing was alight and when he went through the doors soon afterwards, he saw fire at the roof outbye of the fan. Boyd reached the fan shortly before 7.30 am. The fire in the fan itself was still burning but, when he went through the doors, he saw only smouldering in the roadway between the fan and the safety fence, although the return airway was ablaze outbye of the by-pass junction. When Pettigrew went through the three doors a few minutes later, he found fire and a fall of roof at the junction.

There was some uncertainty about the time when hoses and other fire-fighting appliances were taken down the pit, but it emerged that it was 8.00 am, or perhaps a few minutes afterwards. This equipment reached the scene of the fire between 8.20 and 8.30 am and it was quickly put into service by men under the supervision of Pettigrew. At first only one line of hose was used. Much later in the morning, Pettigrew learned that men were trapped in the return airway and he instructed R Harvey, the Safety Officer, to carry out a check of all men in the pit. Harvey did this and then went to the surface, where a similar check had been instituted by the manager, J F Smellie, at about 8.00 am. As a result of these checks, it became apparent that forty seven-men were missing.

Fire fighting continued throughout the day. For some hours, the fire-fighters were able to keep up with the fire, but after a time they were hampered by falls of roof which occurred as the wooden laggings above the girders were burnt away; the strata present in the roadway was naturally oil bearing at some locations in this vicinity.

Action on the Surface

Soon after Pettigrew and McKinnon went down the pit, Kirkpatrick, the pump maintenance man who had learned of the fire at the fan from Thornton, the electrician at the pit bottom, reached the surface with J White, a roadman, and began to assemble hoses and extinguishers. The manager, who had been told of the fire by Pettigrew, prepared to go down the pit; he like Pettigrew and McKinnon had not appreciated that the lives of men were in danger. On his way to the lamp room, however, between 7.20 and 7.25 am, he saw Green being brought out the pit unconscious and recognised that something was very seriously wrong below ground. The manager realised that it was not safe to use the upcast shaft and immediately gave instructions for winding in it to cease. He told White to inform the engineman of the downcast shaft that the needles were to be lifted at once and then to go down the pit himself and see that the lifting operation was carried out properly and quickly. The fire-fighting equipment collected by Kirkpatrick and White had meantime been assembled at the downcast pit-head awaiting the lifting of the needles. The banksman at the pit, T Montgomery, put the time at which White descended a little after 7.35 am, and said that before 8.00 am the needles had been raised and the rope lengths adjusted by a drum clutch to permit winding down to the lower level pit bottom; the manager put this time at 7.55 am, which he calculated by reference to his movements following a call he made to the Rescue Brigade.

Before telephoning the Rescue Brigade, the manager had spoken on the telephone to C M Inglis, the Group Manager, and told him of the fire. The manager gave as the reason for this order of priority the fact that access could not be gained to the No 2 pit workings until the needles in the downcast shaft had been lifted, an operation which would take some 20 minutes.

Thereafter, the Area General Manager and other members of area management, B Spencer, H M Senior District Inspector of Mines and Quarries, and L Cheeseborough, H M District Inspector of Mines and Quarries, were informed of the fire and quickly arrived at the colliery.

Rescue Brigade Operations

The manager's telephone call to the Coatbridge Central Rescue Station was received at the station at 7.40 am.

The first team left the station at 7.45 am and arrived at the colliery, seven and a half miles away, at 8.00 am. This team was comprised of six men - one Instructor and five Brigademen: W Bell, Team Captain, J Armour, H Campbell, J Holmes and I E Savage.

The second rescue team left the station at 7.55 am and arrived at the colliery at 8.10 am; the team members were: A Bridges, H Hamilton, H Gibson, R Drummond, W McAlpine.

The first team was briefed by the manager. R Harvey, Safety Officer, was present. The Superintendent, W K Dyer of the Central Rescue, had now arrived and witnessed the briefing of the Rescue Team. The first team descended the No 1 downcast shaft at 8.08 am and immediately set up a Fresh Air Base (FAB) on the intake air side of the pair of separation air doors, which were adjacent to the large haulage wheel house. This point was the nearest in fresh air, to the man riding haulage roadway.

The first team, wearing self-contained breathing apparatus, of five men, left the FAB at 8.15 am; they made a preliminary inspection of the return roadway in the area where Green had been recovered sometime previously, and they returned to FAB at 8.35 am. They reported to the Superintendent, who had arrived underground, and J Simpson and R Harvey, that they had been unable to see, the atmosphere being very bad with near zero visibility; but they had stumbled upon a body some distance from the base. The second team had now arrived at the FAB underground at 8.33 am. The first team were given instructions by the Superintendent; they were to enter the return roadway again and recover the body they had encountered; this team left the FAB at 8.40 am. The body was recovered, P McMillan, 47 on the plan, to the base at 8.55 am. Artificial respiration was given for a period of 30 minutes by this team, but without success. Dr G Jamieson, the local G P pronounced McMillan dead at 9.25 am at the underground FAB.

The second team was prepared to enter the affected return roadway; they proceeded from the FAB at 9.00 am and returned within fifteen minutes to report that conditions were no better; when they came out the members of the team were in a distressed condition, due mainly to the heat. They were unable to determine the temperature, however, because the atmosphere was so dense that they could not take a reading, except when close to the separation doors where there was some leakage of fresh air. The reaction bands of palladium sulphite tubes used for carbon monoxide determination became completely black, indicating a concentration well in excess of 0.1 per cent (1,000 parts per million). Subsequent analysis of samples of air, collected later by rescue men, showed the presence in the return airway of 0.4 percent carbon monoxide (4,000 p.p.m), a concentration which, with other effects of fire, would have caused death very quickly. The second team members had one change in membership from those already given. D Clark was omitted and his place was taken by R Drummond, Ventilation Officer, Auchengeich Colliery, who was a trained rescue man part-time member. This team was deployed at 9.25 am to the Fire Area at the Fan. The Rescue Superintendent looked into the return airway and decided that conditions were so bad that he was not justified in risking the lives of the members of his team to undertake a full-scale search. The Rescue Team deployed to the fire area, without breathing apparatus, and worked alongside the colliery men, giving advice and valuable assistance generally. When signal bells were heard at about 4.30 pm, colliery workmen, with Rescue Brigademen standing by, started at once to open a way to the return through a stopped-off crosscut; some time later two men broke through into the return, but the atmosphere was such as to confirm conclusively the view, taken much earlier in the day, that there was no conceivable chance of survival for anyone in it. It was subsequently discovered that the bell signals had been caused by falls of roof fouling the haulage signal pull wire in the return airway.

Later at the Fire

The Methane content of the air passing over the fire was continuously watched. The airflow was regulated by varying the openings in door-ways and by erecting sheets at strategic points. In this way the methane content was kept below two per cent. By 9.00 pm the fire fighters, encouraged by an apparent reduction in the smoke, thought they had the fire under control. At Johnston's Crosscut, however, the smoke was found still to be very dense and it was realised that, despite their strenuous efforts, the fire fighters were not overtaking the fire. Some time just before 9.30 pm, R J Evans, H M District Inspector of Mines and Quarries, noticed that a methanometer was recording two and a half percent of methane just outbye the junction of the two return airways. There were percentages approaching four and a half at places in the return airway from the Coking Coal Sections and he quite properly advised the withdrawal of all men to the intake airway. By 10.15 pm the methane content in places was five per cent, and he informed Dr Hyde, H M Divisional Inspector of Mines and Quarries, who was at the surface. With agreement of all parties concerned, everyone in the pit was withdrawn to the surface. Hoses, which had been earlier laid in the downcast pit bottom in readiness for such eventuality, were then brought into use to commence flooding the valleys in the intake and return airways near Johnston's Crosscut, to seal off the fire. (NB The explosive range of methane when mixed with air is between 5 per cent, to 15 per cent).

This flooding of the valleys, in the intake and return airways, at the site took just under 72 hours and was completed at 10.00pm on Monday 21st September. The programme for the recovery of the bodies was now put into operation.

The Recovery of the Bodies

The Personnel

Dr H L Willett, Deputy Director-General of Production, H Q National Coal Board, London (Special Duties regarding Rescue and Recovery at Mines in Great Britain) was now present at the colliery. The Superintendent of Coatbridge Rescue Station, W K Dyer, had made the arrangements for the attendance of forty rescue personnel, both full-time and part-time, to be at the colliery for 9.00 pm on the 21st September. Coatbridge Rescue Station would provide fifteen personnel: two Instructors J Simpson and W Adams, and 12 members of the permanent corps: John Armour, W Aitken, A Bridges, H Campbell, J Campbell, H Gibson, H Hamilton, S Manning, W McAlpine, T Prentice, I E Savage and A Todd. These men formed the underground crew along with the listed part-time rescue men. The part-time rescue men and their parent colliery were as given: Alan Burns, D O'Brien, Robert Drummond, (Auchengeich Colliery), James Armour, Charles Sharkey, (Bedlay Colliery), John Henderson, Adam Gibson, Adam Mann and John Peattie (Cardowan Colliery), William Doolan (Dullatur Colliery), Patrick Higney and James Young (Dumbreck Colliery), Frank Tierney (Garscube Colliery), Patrick Quinn, D.Machray and Edward McAtee (Gartshore 9/11 Colliery), James Eadie (Boglea Colliery), Charles Seaman, (Twechar Colliery) and John Boreland, Chris Ryan (Wester Auchegeich Colliery). There is one person that is not named in the part-time members list now known as G Dempsey (Auchengeich Colliery), a recent transferee from Hamilton Palace Colliery, who resided at Burnbank, Lanarkshire. Robert Barclay, Policy Mine, also attended one day. (NB Robert Drummond was taken off the active list, as he was required for his Ventilation Officer's duties at Auchengeich Colliery during most of the incident). The Surface Rescue Room at the colliery was under the control of W Townsley, Assistant Superintendent, Coatbridge Rescue Station and T Burns of the Permanent Corps at the same Station. The Officer in overall charge of rescue procedures at the incident was W K Dyer, Superintendent of Coatbridge Rescue Station. This station provided immediate cover to the Auchengeich Colliery and the surrounding collieries with the following staff: J Brown, Instructor, and the Permanent Corps of W Bell, A Kirkland, and 3 others sited at the above Station. W Dick, Superintendent Kilmarnock Rescue Station, did relief duties at the colliery.

Recovery Procedure

The recovery procedure was organised in the following manner. The No. 1 downcast shaft was the point of entry into the colliery. The first descent of the winding cage was made without any personnel on board. A lighted flame safety lamp and a canary were fixed to hanging brackets in this cage and suspended in a safe position. The cage was lowered to the lower level pit bottom, very slowly, and rested there for a few minutes, then raised to the surface in the same manner. This shaft had not been in use for three days; a lighted lamp was used to show that sufficient oxygen to sustain life was present; a canary was used to indicate the presence of carbon monoxide. (The flame lamp on the return of the cage to the surface was still lit and the canary was alive on the perch in the Haldane Humane Cage – canary box!).

At 11.00 pm the investigation of the No. 1 shaft and the pit bottom area took place by the rescue personnel. The rescue team entered the return airway for a short distance to take collected air samples; also temperature and humidity checks were made at this point; these results determined the operation time of future recovery rescue teams. The atmosphere at the FAB site, and the immediate return airway adjacent to the air doors was examined thoroughly by the rescue team. Temperature and humidity checks were also made at this site. The personnel who made this inspection were J Simpson, Instructor, Brigademen J

Campbell, H Campbell, J Armour, A Bridges and H Hamilton, with Dr H L Wilett in attendance, in fresh air, with the Instructor at the FAB. The standby rescue team remained on the surface at the top of the No. 1 pit-head. This team was comprised of Brigademen W Adams, W McAlpine, I E Savage, C Sharkey and J Peattie. The inspection team returned to the surface of the colliery at 11.40 pm, and they reported that conditions underground were favourable for the next stage of the recovery; the air samples were analysed at the mobile laboratory sited on the pit-head and staffed by the NCB Scientific Department, Scottish Division. The next stage of the recovery was cleared to go ahead, as soon as possible.

The final inspection commenced at 1.00 am on Tuesday 22nd September. The rescue team that carried out this procedure named W Adams, Team Captain, W McAlpine, J Peattie, C Sharkey and I E Savage. This team, which was fully equipped and wearing self-contained breathing apparatus, entered the return airway and proceeded to the man-riding haulage roadway to try to locate the positions of the missing personnel, some forty-six in number, somewhere in this road. (They were expecting to travel for six hundred yards, if possible, to the top of the 1:5 dipping roadway, providing conditions allowed; the heat and humidity were to be observed closely and related to the safety chart (Lind)).

This rescue team and the standby team proceeded underground, with J Simpson,

Instructor, who would officiate at the FAB., whilst this inspection was taking place. Other officials who were present at this base were D Richards, District Inspector of Mines and Quarries, W K Dyer, Rescue Station Superintendent, Dr Ian Donaldson, Area Medical Officer, NCB Central West Area, Scotland and other colliery officials. The FAB was established at the ventilation doors at the pit bottom of No. 1 shaft, which was the nearest fresh-air point to the return airway. A standby rescue team was sited at this FAB to cover the inspection team.

The inspection team left this FAB at just after 1.00 is. They travelled to a point some one hundred yards inbye, when their head lamps picked up the large reflector on the man haulers front light; although this light was not in operation, its reflector cast an eerie light beam from the team's cap lamps. At this point, a large number of the missing personnel could be seen some distance from the rescue team, as they proceeded towards the bogies. As the team arrived at the train, the team captain started to make a head count of the victims, assisted by I E Savage. W Adams used a notebook to assist him and entered a number in sequence from No. 1 to, hopefully, No. 46. This took some time to accomplish; other team members looked around the train particularly to the adjacent side from Adams and Savage, in case some of the victims were on this opposite side of the train; but at this moment none were located in the area not viewed by the chroniclers. Adams and Savage had now reached a count of 43; with 3 still unaccounted for, a double count was made by the aforementioned, but again the same figure was reached; all these bodies were on the train. The team proceeded inbye from the train and, after travelling a short distance, 2 bodies were found close together, just off the man hauler track rail; 45 victims had now been found, with just one to locate. The rescue team proceeded forward towards the position of the pump shown on the plan; after searching this area, they did not locate the last body, No. 46. This body was not found until two days later, on the 24th of September. The locating of this body will be referred to later in this report. The inspection team now made their return journey to the FAB and arrived back at this base at 2.20 am and the team captain gave his interim report to the officials present; everyone then returned to the surface of the colliery to prepare for the recovery of the bodies, and also to service their breathing apparatus.

At 3.30am, the Rescue Station Superintendent had called a meeting of all the forty rescue men on the site, and their officials. He gave these men a picture of the events found by the inspection team and the difficulties that would be presented to recovery teams. He also stated that if any member did not want to participate in this recovery he would fully understand. It would not affect their future in the Mines Rescue Service. Not one voice was raised; only a slight nod of the head from rescue men of their approval and full participation in the impending recovery of their "mining brothers". Their training and their willingness to help demanded nothing less.

The Superintendent then gave a resume of the make-up of the rescue teams who would undertake the recovery. Eight teams were to be formed and they would comprise of four men in each team, with a designated captain of each one. The first team in operation was to determine how many recovery runs they would make and the number of bodies they could physically recover in the allotted time, whilst wearing breathing apparatus. On each run the team were to carry a stretcher, blanket, length of Hessian brattice sheet, small knife, numbered disc (1-45), and a corresponding numbered disc (1-45) which would be attached to a steel pin 18 inches long.

The stretcher was for the body being recovered to be transported upon. The blanket to cover the body. The Hessian was to wrap any detonator cases found attached to the belts of any bodies; seven shotfirers were still on this train. The wrapped detonator case and its location, was to be placed at the roadside next to where the body was found and reported to HMI at the FAB. These were to be collected later by HMI personnel. The numbered disc and string were to be attached to the clothing on the body. The disc and steel pin were to be driven into the position where the body was lifted.

The eight teams were each captained by a member of the Permanent Corps. This, from the memory of I E Savage, is the list of the team captains and the full-time members with the part-time members taking the vacant places. For accurate list of Team Members of original 8 teams present please consult Jimmy Simpson's Notes available on HEALEY'S HEROES on line.

No   1.   J Campbell (T/Capt),

   2.   I.E Savage (T/Capt), C Sharkey, E McAtee, J Eadie

The recovery teams on their return to the FAB, with a body on each occasion, were to give a report by the captain to the officials at the base, with particular reference to the team's comfort and also the finding of detonators and explosives on the man-rider train. The body would then be transferred by twelve underground workers, who were organized in three groups of four stretcher bearers, who would then convey each body recorded to the Official in charge of No 1 pit bottom. This Official would then organise the transportation of the recovered body to the mortuary on the surface of the mine. (I E Savage cannot remember all of the twelve men involved in this transportation exercise, but four that come to mind were Peter Smith, Jackie Pullen, Peter Starr and Patrick McKeown. All twelve were to carry out a marvellous and highly taxing task; and it would be remiss not to mention that they were workmates, and sometimes close friends, of all the victims of this sad incident. They recognised each of the bodies as they were brought out of the return airway and named them without much delay to the officials at the FAB. This information was used for their records and future official reports. Each of the victims had a personal number attached to their electric cap lamp battery and private personal items on their person which corroborated these workmen's identification of the bodies).

The recovery of the bodies of the victims was commenced at just before 4.00am and the FAB was at the site selected for previous inspections by the rescue teams and was about three hundred yards from the man-riding train. The first team, captained by J Campbell, left the FAB and made three journeys and recovered bodies 1, 2 and 3, as shown on the plan, in a time of thirty minutes, and the team captain indicated that his team were at their physical limitation. This effort by team No 1 set the standard for the remainder of the teams to achieve over the next seven hours. The first team proceeded to the surface for a medical examination by Dr Gooding, Senior Medical Officer, NCB Scotland, assisted by the Senior Nurse from Cardowan Colliery. They then attended to servicing their personal breathing apparatus for their next spell of duty, some three hours hence. Before that they had a light meal at the colliery canteen. This programme of events was undertaken by each of the operational rescue teams. The procedure of recovery by the rescue teams continued unabated until 11.09 am, some seven hours later.

Personal Recollections by I E Savage, Rescue Team Member

"The rescue team designated to me was No 6 team and our first recovery, commenced at just before 7.00 am, was completed at 7.30 am with bodies Nos 16, 17 and 18 recovered; with one shotfirer (17) in this group. After finishing our task, we undertook the same procedure as J Campbell's team and then on to the circulating roster for the next round of duty. The succeeding recovery operation for No 6 team was to commence at 10.15 am and the bodies Nos 40, 41 and 42 recovered with another shotfirer found in this group (42). The team returned to the surface and went through the previous procedure, medical, servicing of BA, light meal; thinking that I was now finished duty, the meal was a little more than light. I had been on duty just over twenty-four hours, with no thought of sleep or even feeling tired. At twenty-three years of age, a desire to see the task completed kept me going through this arduous work, but I still was required for one more occasion at the colliery that day. The last bodies (Nos 43, 44, 45) were recovered by team No 7 at 11.09 am; this part of the recovery was completed and the F.A.B was cleared of buckets of dettol and water; the large elbow length rubber gloves, which were worn for the recovery, were cleaned thoroughly, and put into storage for a few days. The last body (No 46) was recovered in the early hours of Thursday 24th September from the area around the pump shown on the plan. The body was found located under a small roof fall, close to a water lodgement; a coffin was brought underground to assist transporting it to the mortuary on the surface. The mortuary was staffed by a team of morticians and supported by the Glasgow City Police Force. It was sited in the Old Joiners' Workshop, a short distance from No 1 Pit downcast shaft. The above times are only approximations, see Jimmy Simpson's Notes on HEALEY'S HEROES on line. These notes, written by Jimmy, were used for the PUBLIC INQUIRY, which took place at a later date. I would personally like to thank Jimmy's son for making his father's notes available, sometime after we had made these observations.

At 12.30 pm on Tuesday 22nd September, I was informed by W K Dyer, Superintendent, MRS that a further task had to be completed at the man-rider train in the return airway. A full survey of the site had to be undertaken, using a scaled plan of the bogies, and the position of all bodies, which had been recovered, were to be recorded by number at the appropriate position where each body had been located prior to recovery. It was his opinion that, as I had been in the area on a number of occasions (three), I had the experience necessary for him to appoint me as captain of the team to undertake this work. The team was named by him as I E Savage (Team Captain), A Todd, C Seaman, J Eadie and H Gibson. The team went underground with a standby team and Instructor at 12.45 pm and completed the work that is detailed above. The task was quite taxing and not easy to accomplish in fairly dark conditions, being also difficult not too damage the large scroll plan. The team returned to the FAB at 14.10 pm, with the task successfully completed. The detail, which was printed on this plan by the team, was then copied by the colliery surveyor on to a plan for use by the Commissioner in the official report following the Public Inquiry into the Incident at Auchengeich Colliery, which would be published at a later date.

The main rescue activity was scaled down at 15.00 pm on Tuesday 22nd September, but with a small number of Permanent Corps being retained at the colliery for a further ten days. On Friday 25th September, I was again on duty at the Colliery; the funerals of the victims would take place at various locations in the surrounding districts that day, and we would take over duties at the colliery, which would enable their staff to attend these services. The team was W Bell, J Holmes, I E Savage, H Campbell and John Armour. The team arrived at the colliery at 6.10 am, to be underground for 7.00 am to commence cover duties underground. As the team had some time to spare after being briefed by the Colliery management staff, they went to the Old Joiners' Workshop to pay their respects to the victims. 43 coffins were present in this outhouse; 4 of the deceased having been taken to Glasgow Police H Q for a post-mortem to be carried out on them. The Workshop was located a short distance from the Main Office; it was approximately 80 ft in length, 20ft in width and 15 ft in height, with a sloping ridged roof fitted with windows for sufficient light and ventilation. The south wall was fitted with windows along its length. The north wall was also fitted with windows along its length. The north wall and ends were all brick built, as was the south wall below the windows. Other doors which were fitted were closed off for limited access; you entered through this one door; it was like entering a small-scale church building, with a panoramic view in front of you as you viewed this vista of coffins all sitting on individual little trestles. The whole scene was bathed in early morning light with rays of the rising sun penetrating through the roof and sidewall windows. These shafts of light presented a surreal scene, as they seemed to dance on top of each coffin. The coffins had two large floral wreaths placed on top of them, with two plastic bags on the floor beside the coffins containing the deceased's personal belongings. Scenes so touching and at the same time so colourful, but at first sight so sombre and quiet and church like. This site was so respectful and whoever arranged it, with so much dignity, must be respected for his work; it was so professional. I do not think this scene was viewed by the relatives, as they awaited the arrival of their loved one's remains at the various churches. We witnessed it for them and paid our respects that morning. Humbly we present that memorable sight to them for posterity; please may they forever R I P.

On Thursday the 17th September 1959, the

day before this disaster, I was in the company of some of the men who were to lose their lives on that fateful day at Auchengeich Colliery. We were all in attendance at the funeral service of the late J (Tim) Gray, the former Bath Superintendent, who died in service, from Auchengeich Colliery, after illness. The service was held at St. Barbara's Church, Muirhead; just a few miles from the colliery. The colliery had not been in production for some days, due to strike action, but it was due to commence production on the next day, 18th September 1959. It was so ironic and sad; I was to make contact once more with these men, in whose company I was present at the aforementioned funeral service some days previously. Nine victims of the disaster had their pre-burial service held at St Barbara's Church on 25th September 1959. A similar funeral service was held at Chryston Parish Church for some of the victims.

The corn-fields were shrouded in blackness, once again."

Recommendations following Public Inquiry into Underground Fire at Auchengeich Colliery, Lanarkshire, 18th September 1959

1.   Underground booster fans driven by inflammable belts should be constantly attended by competent and properly instructed persons.

2.   The bearings of underground fans should be lubricated with grease or any

suitable non-flammable lubricant that may be developed.

3.   All power transmission belts used at collieries should be made of fire-resistant material. Pending the introduction of fire-resistant flat belting, managers should make effective arrangements to ensure that over-heating or fire in machinery driven by inflammable belt will be discovered and dealt with before serious danger can develop.

4.   All managers should carry out thorough reviews of their fire-fighting arrangements to ensure that sufficient appliances in proper working order, will be available for prompt use in any place where fire may break out underground. These reviews should include consideration of telephone systems and means of warning men of fire.

5.   All managers should have thorough examinations made of the whole of their pits to identify any places of unusually high fire-risk at each of these places and to deal with any fire which may occur.

6.   The Attention of all officials should be drawn specifically to their obligation under Regulation 11 (1) of the Coal and other Mines (Fire and Rescue) Regulations, 1956, that men must be withdrawn as soon as there is any indication that fire has, or may have, broken out below ground.

7.   The industry should reconsider its decision to discontinue the trials of self-rescuers.

8.   There should be a suitably constituted standing committee of experts representing all

side of the Industry and Ministry of Power, charged with the task of keeping under close and constant review the prevention of explosions and fires in mines, with particular reference to the lessons of actual fires and explosions in this country and abroad, and of anticipating any possible ignition hazards arising or likely to arise from new developments in mining practice. NB Self-rescuers are small breathing units capable of filtering carbon monoxide following a fire or explosion underground.

I E SAVAGE
June 2008

Sources: Ministry of Power - Underground Fire at Auchengeich Colliery,
        Lanarkshire, 18th September 1959 - CMND 1022
                Glasgow Herald
                Glasgow Evening Times
                I E Savage - Personal Notes

Names of Men Killed in the Fire

Name	Age	Ref No Plan
Alexander Morrison Beattie	26	29
Thomas Bone	27	12
Francis Broadley	38	44
William Brynes	54	33
Mathew Mcilwain Cannon	38	28
Walter Clark	61	26
Henry Clayton	62	1
Robert Conn	30	10
Andrew Crombie	42	39

James Devine	39	36
Andrew White Docherty	43	8
John Duffy	39	22
Francis Jones Fisher	49	17
Martin Fleming	51	35
Michael Fleming	47	42
Richard Hamilton	48	41
James Harvey	44	40
Patrick Harvey	33	2
Edward Henery	61	14
George Jackson	21	9

Francis Kiernan	26	3
Peter Kelly	40	24
William Lafferty	39	32
Alexander Todd Lang	35	6
William Leishman	56	31
Gerald John Martin	34	19
John McAuley	42	16
Robert McCoid	55	18
Joseph McDonald	53	5
Denis McElhaney	49	45

George Thomas T McEwan	20	7
George Wilkie McIntosh	58	34
Andrew McKenna	41	43
Peter McMillan	55	47
James McPhee	54	27
William Meechan	22	13
John Muir	38	37
John Mulholland, Senior	50	4
James Nimmo	32	25
Aaron Price	50	46
Robert Price	47	15

Alexander Sharp	34	30
John Shevlin	46	23
William Skilling	53	38
John Mack Stark	23	20
Thomas Stokes	32	11
Donald Cameron Weir	30	21

Black Gold

*Connecting with families and friends
from around the world*

In words...

Since the Black Gold launch we have received numerous emails and letters from those who are now back in touch after decades apart. Since the disaster in 1959, few stayed at home and never ventured far away from the colliery and others spread far and wide. It is part of nature that people move away for all sorts of reasons but you can bet work played its part for the travellers. We got in touch with people from all over the United Kingdom to far away places like Australia and Canada. It was quite amazing to have some great conversations from those who were there that day or were connected in so many ways to one of the country's worst disasters.

From Canada

Rita McNaughton *(nee McMurray)* gave the Black Gold project her connected story with the disaster with some very personal touching moments that involved one of her family members. Rita worked in Lewis' department store in the offices. Raised by her Mum after her father passed away in October, 1954. She had five brothers and four sisters. The fourth born was John McMurray, who would later on go onto enjoy life working as a Priest. John was ordained on June 24th, 1958 at the cathedral in Motherwell. St Barbara's R.C. Church in Muirhead was Father John's first parish.

John would be given the role of administering the rights of the Catholic Church to the miners who had sadly passed away. Clearly at this stage there were still safety concerns but Father John's only concern was to give those miners their rights that they so richly deserved.

As a young Priest at the time, this was an extraordinary experience and Father John, at the time of the disaster was only in his mid-twenties. Even although John was a Priest, he was humble; he came from that area and was from a large family but being a Priest didn't make it any easier – he was just the same as everybody else.

After his spiritual assignment John was given a week's break; it was more like a recovery. He found it very difficult to talk to the families about his role in administering the rights to their loved ones.

"Everybody wants to go to Heaven but no-one wants to die."

Father John passed away on June 3rd, 2001.

From the USA

Alison Schuchs from the USA has a special connection to the Auchengeich Colliery disaster. She told the Black Gold project via email: "My father always spoke about the Auchengeich disaster but I didn't realize he was meaning to write a book about it. When my Dad passed away I was going through his things and he had lots of notes he had taken from miners who had survived. Fortunately for us my Dad missed the terrible accident as he was in hospital at the time. He could well have been killed, also."

Alison Schuchs
Daughter of William Walker McLean

From Australia

Trish Borgogno told us about her connection. She wrote: "My Father Samuel Barr *(known as Sam)* was working at Auchengeich at the time of the disaster – he was in the other shaft. The disaster happened two days before my parents' first anniversary and my Mother was five months pregnant with my stster, Dorothy Barr, Katie and Robert Barr were my grandparents. My parents immigrated to Australia in 1964, moving to the Nickel Mines in Kalgoorlie, Western Australia. Robert Barr still lives in Stepps.

Closer to home the Black Gold project received great support and contributions from many others who have a special connection to the disaster:

Archie Downie

I worked in the Bedlay Pit and was in Gartcosh Iron Mills at 19-years-old when that fateful day occurred. I went to the pit and attended the scene when they brought up our mates. They were even dragging water out of the burns to put down the pit and the area was like a deathly silence; although there were many, many people who had gathered including the Salvation Army and the Food Services who provided food and sustenance. There were a lot of my friends down there never to be forgotten. My heart, along with others, bled for them.

Bill Ewing

I was an apprentice engineer at Auchengeich and 18-years-old at the time of the disaster. I have attended every memorial service since they started and the memories of that fateful day will stay with me forever.

I was on the surface and witnessed Peter McMillan and Tam Green being taken from the cage to the ambulance room. I also remember arriving at the pit and remarking about the smell of smoke. It was a terrible morning.

I knew a lot of the men who died. Most of the engineering staff had been paid off because the miners were on strike and being an apprentice I was working along with the engineers on safety cover. I had been on the site of the fan just a few days prior to it going on fire. Again, it is a memory which has given me many a nightmare.

I also believe the brave men who risked their lives and went into the smoke to rescue their comrades should be given some kind of decoration for their bravery. They were mentioned in the inquiry but never fully recognized.

Carol Quinn

My Dad, Billy Quinn, was there that day the disaster happened. He was supposed to be on the last bogey that went down but decided to finish his cigarette first. Lucky for him but sadly, forty-seven men lost their lives.

My Dad came from Moodiesburn and my Mum from Cardowan. He lost his brother-in-law, Alec Lang, and other relatives too.

I do remember seeing a newspaper clipping with my Dad's sister on the front page. Auntie Margaret lost her husband, Alec Lang and Auntie Mary lost her husband, M Fleming.

Joanne Reilly

My father *(Arthur Kelly)* was working in Cardonald Colliery in 1959 and was Fire Officer and First-Aider and volunteered to help bring up the bodies of the men killed.

He always spoke of the tragedy of the men

killed with respect and sadness as it obviously distressed him *(he was only 20-years-old at the time although had been a miner for nearly four years).*

I think we sometimes forget the men who do this important and traumatic job, especially in that particular time when tough miners where not suppose to be 'soft'. Although, as most people will admit, my Dad was a big softie at heart, as I suppose most of the families of the men who died would say about their fathers, too.

Liz Cullen

Liz Cullen's *(nee Milligan)* granddad survived the disaster by crawling with the others to another part of the site. She was almost 7-years-old and on holiday in Rothsay when her Dad Neil Milligan heard it on the radio. She added: "Our cases were packed immediately and we were down at the ferry port inside half-an-hour."

Liz's Uncle Joe Milligan worked at Bedlay Pit and lived right beside Auchengeich and rushed over to help.

Robert Armour

I have strong links with Auchengeich as my father John Armour was a member of the First Mines Rescue Team to enter the pit on the day of the disaster. My uncle James went in with the Second Team.

My family all have strong links with the

mining community living in Moodiesburn, Chryston, Mountellen, etc, and many of my uncles were miners.

I feel like Auchengeich is woven into the fabric of my life, as for many years after the disaster was discussed and talked about. Although I probably didn't really know what they were talking about, it all makes sense now I read all the information and accounts.

I am a songwriter and wrote a song *'Mines Rescue Man'*, which is a tribute to my Dad and the Mines Rescue Teams.

Tom McLelland

My uncle, James Harvey, died in the Auchengeich mining disaster. He left a widow, my aunt Alice *(my mother's sister)* and several children who were our cousins.

I was not aware of the 50 year commemoration but have been reading about it recently. I well remember at the time, in the day after the disaster I read the list of fatalities in the morning newspaper and was shocked to read of James Harvey's death. I think I was about 13-years-old.

We were all miners. My grandfather and father worked in Cardowan Colliery; my two brothers and myself all worked in Plean Collieries, Stirlingshire. I left the NCB in 1964 and joined the army to travel the world, like a lot of miners did.

It left a big hole in the family I remember, but as with all mining communities, family and friends rallied and pulled together.

I have not had any contact with James Harvey's family over the past 35 years or so but my memories of visiting them every year for the summer school holidays *(and vice versa)* remain with me to this day.

It was a very sad day for Lanarkshire, Scotland and the mining industry and we should forever remember how much miners and their families have given for the country.

Lasting note

Fate played a huge part in the lives of the miners and their families on the blackest day on the 18th September, 1959. Few have moved on with their lives but none will ever forget the day that forty-seven men left their houses and families to begin what was supposed to be a *normal* day's work. That was certainly not the case as forty-seven brave men and their families were to find out – at a huge cost.

The Black Gold project also learned from our meetings and correspondence with ex-Miners and families of the deceased miners, so many lessons and we tried to capture, as best we could, a project that would be fitting for so many brave men who worked dangerously each shift so that the country could enjoy a warm home in the cold, hard, winter days and nights. Those men and their work can never, and should never, be overlooked or underestimated. We often speak about heroes today, and there are many, but forty-seven heroes passed on to the other side that terrible day in 1959.

Fate played a huge part the other way in many examples. George Elliott's motorbike broke down on the way to the pit that morning otherwise he would have been on the second bogey load. Fate took a terrible twist for the families. You just cannot begin to feel what they must have been going through from the moment the news filtered through to the agonizing waiting. Those poor people must have been through hell and back again. It is for those people that this book was constructed in such a way; to let them have their say and if anything we hope the information has at least some comfort or closure in many respects.

Throughout our research we read some brilliant drafts and heard some great songs. Danny O'Connor wrote the extremely impressive novel, *The Honest Heart,* a moving tribute to the forty-seven men who sadly lost their lives in the disaster. We heard songs, read poems and poured over the many emails of people who were there. It has been an extraordinary journey filled with deep emotion. We also had people who didn't want to give their account and we can understand that. The grief of that day was too much and still hard to talk about for many and naturally we respect that.

A very special thanks to all the contributors to the Black Gold book; if not for you this book would not have been possible.

Lastly and more importantly, a very special and respectful thanks to the forty-seven men who worked extremely hard in difficult and dangerous surroundings. Their work so often goes unrecognized but not any longer. It was those brave men and many like them who risked their lives every time they went to work and we can never, ever, forget that.

For the humble ones who worked and helped tremendously on the Black Gold project; we are all in agreement with one full lesson we have all taken from working on this tribute book to forty-seven heroes and that is:

We shall never see their likes again.

This book is a dedication to the forty-seven men who died in one of Scotland's worst disasters on the 18th of September, 1959.

R.I.P.

A publication by Black Gold
For more information please visit:
www.blackgoldonline.co.uk

www.ingramcontent.com/pod-product-compliance
Lightning Source LLC
La Vergne TN
LVHW051255080426
835509LV00020B/2992